T3-BNM-845

Dorothy L. Sayers

A Pilgrim Soul

Dorothy L. Sayers

A PILGRIM SOUL

Nancy M. Tischler

John Knox Press
ATLANTA

FERNALD LIBRARY
COLBY-SAWYER COLLEGE
NEW LONDON, N.H. 03257

PR
6037
A95
Z9

4/81 Hoffman 8.06

Unless otherwise indicated, all Scripture quotations in this book are from the Revised Standard Version Bible, copyright 1946, 1952, and © 1971, 1973 by the Division of Christian Education, National Council of the Churches of Christ in the U.S.A., and are used by permission.

Library of Congress Cataloging in Publication Data
Tischler, Nancy Marie Patterson.
Dorothy L. Sayers, a pilgrim soul.

Bibliography: p.
Includes index.
1. Sayers, Dorothy Leigh, 1893–1957. 2. Authors, English—20th century—Biography. 3. Scholars—England—Biograpy. I. Title.
PR6037.A95Z9 823'.912 [B] 79-87739
ISBN 0-8042-0882-4

82411

© Copyright John Knox Press 1980
10 9 8 7 6 5 4 3 2 1
Printed in the United States of America
Atlanta, Georgia 30308

But one man loved the pilgrim soul in you,
And loved the sorrows of your changing face.

William Butler Yeats,
"When You Are Old"

For Merle
and Eric
and Grant—

Acknowledgments

I am grateful to the many scholars who have shared their ideas on Dorothy L. Sayers through their conversations, public lectures, articles, and books. Margaret P. Hannay, Alzina Dale Stone, Ralph E. Hone, Bonnie L. Heintz, James Brabazon, Joe Christopher, Roderick Jellema, and Janet Hitchman—as well as numerous others—have all provided me with insights, corrected my interpretations, and added to my knowledge. *The Sayers Review* and the many publications of the Dorothy L. Sayers Literary and Historical Society of Witham have also been enormously helpful. My special thanks to R. L. Clarke and his family for their hospitality at Roslyn House and their help. I am also grateful to Dr. Clyde S. Kilby and the staff of the Wade Collection at Wheaton College for their courtesy and encouragment and help.

I thank the Rev. Aubrey Moody for granting permission to use his words; to David Higham Associates, Ltd. for use of materials from *Further Papers on Dante, The Just Vengeance,* and *Paradise*; and to Armitage Watkins for permission to use lines from *Hangman's Holiday* and *The Zeal of Thy House.*

My deepest gratitude must go to Dr. Barbara Reynolds, who through her lectures, conversations, and letters has clarified and enlivened so much of the literature for me.

In addition, I am appreciative of the Research Council and the Humanities Program of the Capitol Campus of the Pennsylvania State University who provided support for my research and travel.

And, of course, I thank my family, who have patiently endured my mania—these several years—for Dorothy L. Sayers.

Contents

Introduction

By almost any measurement, Dorothy Leigh Sayers was one of the giants of the first half of the twentieth century. As a scholar, a writer, and a public speaker, she excelled. The reluctance of her world to grant her appropriate acclaim is partly because of the very diversity and character of her accomplishments.

I first came to admire her when I discovered her translation of *The Song of Roland.* Her introduction to that work is a masterpiece of thoughtful and witty scholarship. She makes the characters live for us and, in her comments, arouses our laughter at our own time-bound habits. Thousands of other American teachers have been even more delighted with her translation of *The Divine Comedy* and her voluminous notes and essays on the work. Hundreds of teachers and thousands of young readers in American and British colleges have studied Dante through Sayers. Mystery-story addicts, many of whom do not even know of her scholarship, enjoy her for Lord Peter Wimsey and Montague Egg and the three collections of *The Omnibus of Crime.* Her introductions to these collections are basic texts for study of the genre of detective fiction. The English public know her for her radio broadcasts during World War II, her plays over BBC, and her numerous speeches and letters to the editors of various papers. Religious folk know her liturgical dramas. And feminists know her for her book *Are Women Human?* and for her uncompromising life.

But in a sense she was no fixed part of any group. Though a scholar, she did not live or teach in a university town. Though a Christian, she had numerous quarrels with the hierarchy and organizations of her church. Though a popular writer, she heaped scorn on the values of the marketplace.

Hers was a pilgrim soul, restless and striving. Her hunger for all of human experience led her into great pain and great joy. Her searching intellect never settled for received opinion; her appetite for knowledge was not satisfied with easy victories. Like a Renaissance man, she sought knowledge in all fields. Nothing human was foreign to her. Yet she seldom left England, never sought to see much of the physical world. For her, the real adventure was the journey of the inquiring mind.

Hers was an examined life—and one well worth living. Her approach to life (which I have sought to follow in this study) was to dig deep into immediate reality, to search beyond the surface facts of her temporal existence to the universal and transcendent meanings they might image forth. She always insisted on her privacy, always protected her own life from public gaze. Though she used her experience and her personality in developing her characters, she asserted that these fictional creatures were free, not simply puppets or self-portraits. She was *not* Lord Peter, she noted. Though she too loved medieval manuscripts, she did not share his taste in brandy. The private life of the author, the private and individual facts of that life, are irrelevant, she insisted. What she wanted the world to know and what she thought worth knowing, she put in her public statements—her books, speeches, plays, and articles. Yet these public documents are meditations on her own life and world. As she expressed it, her profession was the " 'diabolic occupation of going to and fro in the world' " and asking questions in it.[1]

The progress of this pilgrim and her meditations on her pilgrimage can help—and have helped—other thoughtful people to find meaning in their lives. A twentieth-century English woman faces many of the same monsters as a seventeenth-century English man. Dorothy L. Sayers' landscape at first seems tamer than John Bunyan's, less peopled with monsters and perils. But on closer examination, we find her monsters more subtle and her perils more confusing than his. Threats do indeed challenge the lonely pilgrim seeking her way to the Celestial City. The Wicket Gate, the Slough of Despond, Vanity Fair, the Valley of the Shadow, the Castle of Giant Despair, and the Delectable Mountains are all there for her. She too meets Talkative and Evangelist and Apollyon. She is no gentle Christiana, following meekly with her children in her husband's footsteps. She is Christian himself—as lonely and as threatened and as triumphant as he. We come to love her, not for the volume of her work or the color of her personality, but for her pilgrim soul.

I. Pilgrim of the Intellect

On October 14, 1920, Dorothy Leigh Sayers, aged 27, stood proudly among the first women ever to be granted degrees from Oxford University. Oxford had been allowing women to attend lectures for half a century (properly chaperoned and unobtrusively seated, of course) and had for half that time allowed them to be examined. But when, in 1915, Dorothy L. Sayers completed her studies in modern languages, taking a coveted first in her examinations, she was awarded no diploma, only a "title to a degree." Oxford did not admit women to degree status.

She had been born at Oxford in 1893, the daughter of the Headmaster of the Christchurch Cathedral Choir School, Reverend Henry Sayers. She had been a precocious child, an excellent, natural student of languages—starting Latin at six, or "rising seven" in her phrase. (It was unusual for a girl to study Latin at all.) She was accomplished in French soon after, and then in German as well. She had been a talented and imaginative scholar, an eager learner. Her family, not benighted by Victorian notions about a woman's place, had expected her to win a scholarship to Somerville College at Oxford, and probably expected her to take a first. They may well have expected too that she would become a scholar-teacher.

But history intervened, choking off some channels, opening up others. By the time she became Master of Arts, she had already rejected the tempting life of the scholar and elected the life of the "feeling intellect." She had determined that she must not succumb to the conformity of schoolteaching or the passionate celibacy of the traditional scholar, but must "go hence and seek [her] . . . own renown."[1]

At birth, we are thrust willy-nilly into a world we never chose, full of complex problems and impossible decisions. A girl child born near the end of Victoria's reign, for example, inherited the ambitions and frustrations of the "new women" who, though still without a vote, had at last the chance to own property and to enter college and choose a career. Contrasted with a rector's daughter at the beginning of the nineteenth century (like Jane Austen) or later (the Brontes), Dorothy L. Sayers was born into a time of opportunity. But the rising expectations were doomed to result in disappointment and frustration because of the precise but illogically prescribed limits of life and because of the constant backward tug of tradition. Like Mary Ann Evans (George Eliot), Dorothy L. Sayers was to find the woman of great intellect and small beauty to be held in low esteem. For such a woman, the traditional role of gracious and apparently mindless object of masculine desire and comfort was both a disappointment and an affront. To know one's intellectual and spiritual worth and to be rejected for the shape of one's body, the thickness of one's glasses, or the thinness of one's hair is a shocking outrage.

From the beginning, the girl seems to have realized that she was no beauty. Her round face, long neck, and large bony structure were pleasant enough, but they did not fit the contemporary specifications for the feminine ideal. She seems not to have worried about a corseted torso and a wasp waist. After an illness in her teens, she was further cursed with semi-baldness, a situation that increased her sensitivity and her daring. Her impressive stature and stentorian voice virtually forced her to be authoritative rather than docile. Predictably, among her best creations are women who lament their plainness and finally learn to live with it. The young Hilary in *The Nine Tailors* who is a misfit among the country folk, the female artists in Bloomsbury, the spinsters in Miss Climpson's "cattery" all share a sense of self-doubt, and alienation from their society. Not all can verbalize their discontent, but they sense they are being judged harshly by the wrong standards. Harriet Vane, Sayers' writer-heroine who steals Lord Peter's heart, develops a self-assurance and an individual style that give the impression of handsome appearance without the real thing.

Dorothy L. Sayers was always a person with deep feelings. Her mental alertness was balanced by an emotional intensity. In the early years, though she seems to have loved and admired her mother (a grandniece of Percival Leigh, well known for writing "The Professor" column of *Punch*), she was primarily devoted to her father. He was a quiet, gentle, scholarly man, religious but not evangelical. James Brabazon, Sayers' official biographer, tells us that he was inclined to believe his daughter would develop her faith by "propinquity" rather than indoctrination. He was no great preacher. His shyness encouraged affectionate response in his only child; as a teacher he recognized the girl's talents; and as a scholar he could guide her quick mind. He seems never to have resented the absence of a son; but he did want his daughter to have the advantages a son would have, so he educated her as he would have done a boy. This very benefit must have made adjustment to the larger world difficult for the young girl, for her father was a rare man.

Her only recorded quarrel with him was not on the issue of women's rights but of Latin studies. She insisted he erred, not in starting her so young with classical languages, but in beginning with a "dead" language. She came to believe that medieval Latin was more exciting and relevant than classical—because of its use as the language of theology and debate—and more tempting for the growing child. In an essay entitled "The Lost Tools of Learning" she describes the ideal education, one probably very close to her own. It would adapt the medieval trivium to the appropriate stages of the developing child. Thus, the early, rote stage of life—what she calls the "Poll parrot" stage—is a good time for learning the rules of grammar. The more argumentative stage—the "Pert" stage, she called it—would be an excellent time for teaching the tools of argumentation and logical thought. The last stage—when the adolescent becomes "Poetic"—would be the time to teach rhetoric. It was a period of upheaval in education, with great arguments challenging the value of a liberal education for a scientific age. Dorothy L. Sayers, largely because of her own experience of a classical liberal education, was squarely in the camp of Matthew Arnold and Cardinal Newman. A neo-medievalist in her desire to reconstruct the mind-set of the Middle Ages and translate it for the modern world, she was to stand in the tradition of T. S. Eliot, Charles Williams, and C. S. Lewis.

From Reverend Henry Sayers and from her home life, she came by an early love for Oxford, with its tradition of disinterested learning, for the English church, with its dignified form and architecture, and for culture—especially books and music.

An artist with Dorothy L. Sayers' kind of imagination takes the stuff of her life and transforms it into art. She was four years old when her family moved from their comfortable life in Oxford to Bluntisham Rectory in the fen country. Here she came to understand the town without the gown—the small English village. Her sense of place was always vivid, and this life in the fen country especially informs two of her books, *The Nine Tailors* and *Busman's Honeymoon.* Though they were written years later, after most of her triumphs in detective fiction, they represent her mature reconsiderations of these early years in exile from Oxford. Even as a small child, she sensed the change from the busy university town full of gowned scholars, music, and conversation, to the small market town surrounded by open fields and lonely farms.

The small English village, Dorothy Sayers discovered, with its established roles and set patterns, has its charm and security. Even after her success as a novelist, she chose to divide her life between the village (Witham, just outside London) and the city, not content to live permanently in the midst of the metropolis. Among the numerous roles in this ancient social establishment, the vicar fits as a middle figure—neither landed aristocrat nor simple tradesman. He works with his mind like the doctor, but he heals the spirit rather than the body. Like the doctor, he may be one of the few educated men in the community.

Dorothy's father was an Oxford man (Magdalen College), but was humble in his scholarship. He used his schoolroom in the rectory to teach innumerable young men on their way to public schools (known in America as private schools) or preparing for examinations. He was never wealthy, though some of the vicarages were impressive in size and architecture. (Bluntisham is a lovely Georgian country house in a dignified setting.) But he was the sort of Christlike man who would give another man his own living because his need was greater. Thus, the family, which included a maiden aunt as well as Dorothy and her mother, eventually moved to smaller and poorer parishes, ending at Christchurch, near Wisbech, a community of "eight hundred souls."

The vicars in Sayers' books echo this gentle unworldly man. They concern themselves with the church building, its bellows, arches, roof, and windows. Though versed in Scripture and in theology, they are more inclined to discuss bell ringing or church music than their faith. Their religion is conformist and satisfying, though not to an infrequent chapelgoer, who insists that the up-down-up-down liturgy has more movement than meaning and the sermon has "no 'eart in it." Yet, in time of need, the vicars show Christian sympathy and generosity and forgiveness and love.

Dorothy Leigh Sayers acknowledges the value of this placid bucolic faith and loves the ongoing ritual of the visible church. She respects the order it brings to the life of the community, but she insists on the concurrent deeper religion as well, one with more anarchy and passion. Christ, she noted in an early poem, is the "bonny outlaw" who seeks people out individually—like the lover in a ballad—and lures them away from the herd. Her love of the metaphysical poets and her imitations of them show her taste for fire and passion in religion. The rector who served her in her later years has been quoted as saying she was a fairly regular churchgoer, but inclined to go to eight o'clock services. He notes that this was the service for social misfits who want to be with God in church, but not bothered with other worshipers. Certainly this tension between the established, visible church, and a passionate invisible one continued to characterize her thought throughout her life. In theology, she was an Anglo-Catholic—a nice balance between her medievalism and her patriotism.

An early play, published shortly after her school years at Oxford, portrays and is called *The Mocking of Christ.* Among the tormentors are modern clergymen and bureaucrats, who offer Christ tea and bind him in red tape. As she was later to say, others have blasphemed and persecuted Christ, but it is the Christians who have managed to make him dull. They take the "'eart" out of him with their reduction of God enfleshed to a rationale for middle-class respectability. Their religion is as rote as the fixed prayers they recite, their sense of sin as lifeless as the litanies they mouth. Miss Climpson, Lord Peter's helper, is a passionate soul who can feel the rich experience embodied by the service. And Lord Peter, a less vocal Christian, can sift the words for their meaning and wonder how many of the worshipers truly seek to worship. But the majority of the congregation appear to enjoy the ritual without plumbing its depths. These are the very natural insights of a bright and sensitive youngster who has spent hours listening to services and watching the grotesque ways of the congregation. But of such unlikely stuff is the visible church composed.

One of the real values of reducing the passionate faith to a ritual religion is the preservation of ideas. Sayers was an intellectual Christian, who loved the subtle play of theology and the logic of the church fathers. The service of the church, its ritual recitation of creed, reinforces the essentials of faith. The only begotten Son of God did enter human life, fully human, fully divine. He did live in the flesh like us, did suffer and did die for us, taking on himself our sins. He did rise again from the dead in his new and physical body, and he does sit on the right hand of God from whence he will judge us. In work after work, Sayers returns to the value of the Nicene Creed and the battle for orthodoxy. As a person thrilled with ideas and motivated by them, she cannot excuse wrong thinking or fuzzy logic. She insists on the necessity for the correct structure of thought and faith as the framework for emotional commitment. Her own intensity continued to grow and deepen throughout her life, but never to shift from her original foundations, which were firmly fixed in rock.

Just as the church building, composed of rotting timbers, crumbling stone, and peeling paint, houses and outlasts most of the worshipers within it, so does the visible church community, with all its flaws, outlast the individuals who form it. The continuity of the body of believers is a miracle of such regularity in our history that we notice it only when it falters. Sayers was later to explore the amazing choice Christ made in the foundation of his church—on the fallible and lovable Simon Peter.

Thus, though she laughs gently at the Reverend Simon Goodacre (in *Busman's Honeymoon*), and his silly wife, with their sherry and cocktail biscuits and his "morbid" love of cacti, she realizes that such people as this are the rock on which Christ has chosen to build his church. (The fact is, she loved cacti and sherry herself.)

In parallel manner, the workers of the community, the Twittertons and Puffetts, Kirks, and MacBrides, are essential to the society. The organist, the gardener, the chimney sweep, the policeman, and the schoolteacher—each has an assigned role in the community—a proper work. This ordered society, of which Lord Peter is himself an integral part, provides an atmosphere of security that Dorothy (and Harriet) knew as children.[2] It is certainly the basis of the traditional English society and reinforces a tacit acceptance of the Great Chain of Being.

Roderick Jellema has summed up this set of assumptions by noting that it is a "queer world" Dorothy L. Sayers takes the measure of—"whether you mean to or not, you inherit some of the sophisticated assumptions of this oddity our modern world, some of its rituals, beliefs, myths, ways of looking at things."[3] She did inherit the complex ideas of Oxford, but she also grew to maturity in the simple life of Bluntisham Rectory. This endowed her with an earthiness and directness rare among scholars.

For example, she tells of reading in a children's magazine an article in a series called *Tales from Herodotus* ("or something of that kind") in which she found a picture of Cyrus in a tunic like classical heroes. Having neatly pigeonholed him in her mind with Greeks and Romans, she was startled to realize "with a shock as of sacrilege, that on that famous expedition he had marched clean out of our Herodotus and slap into the Bible."[4] As a child, she came to a rare integration of knowledge, to the acceptance of Scripture as history, not as fairy tale, to a discovery of ideas for herself. This suggests a subtle blending of Oxford reading with fen-country reality. She was later to study about comparative religion, higher criticism, and mythic interpretation. But she started with literal belief.

The lonely old rectories in which Dorothy spent her childhood, isolated from children of her own ability or age, and the churches in which her father served, became the unconscious setting for her maturing imagination. The loneliness encouraged her to read the scores of children's books, the novels, and the detective stories in the house.

Later, in *The Nine Tailors*, she was to catch the mood of the beautiful old churches of the fen country with their mix of Norman, early English, transitional, and perpendicular architecture. The heritage shaped in the abbeys, altered by Henry VIII and again by Cromwell, neglected by the "enlightened" century's folk, and finally restored by the Victorians, bears testimony to the generations who have lived with these buildings they loved without fully appreciating or understanding them. An occasional antiquarian might note the splendor of an angel roof, but the day-to-day users of the parish church were more likely to nail the Christmas decorations right into the antique wood without concern for the consequent damage to the carvings and the finish. Yet these parishioners did understand, as the rector's sensitive daughter would, the moods of the old building in different seasons and different lights. They knew the bells by name and quickly read their messages of death or danger or celebration. They respected their powers and believed their somber mythic histories. The bell tower, the chambers, the roof, the closets, the niches, the graveyard all must have become familiar haunts of the child. (Ironically, Sayers did not discover the science of bell ringing until later years, and had to return to some of the churches to correct her impressions. Even she could not write from memory alone.) Her education was not simply in her father's library and schoolroom, but in the Gothic churches, dark and majestic, where she heard the music of Bach and Handel, the words of the church fathers, and the lessons of Scripture.

The great churches of the fen country are soaring and majestic. The landscape, by contrast, is flat and barren. The floods and "blows" make it dangerous and lonely, not a spot most folk would choose to live. This "beastly country" breeds an independent, serious people who believe in the value of good work and who give their talents eagerly to the Lord. They are suspicious of outsiders and of change, preferring blunt, straightforward speech to flourishes. Like Ruskin's medieval craftsman, they are conscientious and creative in their limited ways. They are eager to learn the complex pattern of change ringing and to give their time to the work.

The country teaches them toughness and industry. The flat land rolls out mile after mile with solitary windmills standing starkly on the barren farms. Dykes and hedges intersect the flat land like squares on a chessboard. It is no country to breed romantic love of nature. The blows bring the floods, sending the folk scurrying to the highest ground, the churchyard, where they huddle during the storm, only to return, in time, to their relentless drudgery.

The remarkable grandeur of the church building, firmly planted on the highest ground as refuges in time of trouble, withstanding the ravages of nature, escaping the perils of war, becomes a powerful symbol of God's enduring strength. Its great tower and arches, firmly rooted in the soil, point heavenward. It houses the church militant during its clumsy and beautiful services, and blesses the church triumphant in its graveyard. Pastors come and go, families live and die, windows are broken and replaced, but the faith withstands the changes.

As Dorothy Sayers grew older and faced more complex problems and deeper pain, she continued to center her life in her faith. As Jellema notes, "broadly knowledgeable about the complexities of our condition, she is increasingly dazzled by the simple story of the world that broke in the first century A.D."[5] In the back of her mind, with all the modern world's complexities, was the chessboard pattern of the fen country with the enduring symbol of faith rising miraculously out of it. However complicated the twentieth century sought to make life for the modern woman, the Christian church could provide the framework for discovering the answers. It was like the grid of the dykes, or the plumb line of God.

The touch of the earth—the reality of the people within the church, with their dirty boots and clumsy words—broke always into her mystic and poetic meditations. Lord Peter is not the only worshiper to notice the crunch of coal when his mind should be on the service or to meditate on the roof design rather than the sermon. These touches of common humanity underscore the remarkable power of the liturgy, which allows us to wander and to return, alternating between human thoughts and veneration of God. The mingling of human and divine pictured here is even more brilliantly illuminated in *The Man Born to Be King*, when Dorothy L. Sayers notes the wonder of God's humanity in Christ, his entrance into human history by way of a peasant girl in a stable. The meditations of a schoolgirl were, in time, to flower into an understanding of the incarnation.

In the schoolroom of the rectory, among the battered lesson books, the growing child absorbed history and geography and languages from the governesses with their "straight-fronted corsets and high-necked frocks with bell sleeves, who wore their hair *à la* Pompadour."[6] Supplementing the education of the father, they taught the child until she was fifteen, and ready (they thought) to go off to a proper boarding school with other young ladies.

After the individual attention of this tutorial system, any class of more than five would have been painful. The shy, awkward teenager went off to the Godolphin School in Salisbury, where she dazzled the others with her language facility, discovered her weakness in math, took part in a house play, and after a year had a breakdown. Janet Hitchman, her first biographer, notes that she started at the wrong time of year, had few friends, and was upset by her poor preparation in math. Ivy Phillips recalls that she was a lonely, egocentric girl, not especially interested in the activities of the other girls—especially not sports. Miss Phillips, remembering a world before World War I, notes that the young women at the school were still children, wearing their hair in pigtails, neatly dressed in their uniforms. They talked mostly about games, work, hobbies, and teachers. Having no real interest in games and sharing few interests with her classmates, Dorothy Sayers was undoubtedly lonely.[7]

After the first year, she was stricken with a disastrous attack of measles, causing her hair to fall out, and leaving her with a choice among a wig, a turban, or a bald head. Showing considerable courage, she slapped a square-cut wig on her head and returned to school, but was shortly to collapse in a nervous breakdown, which forced her to return home. Though she never broke so completely under stress again, she learned sympathy with nervous weakness. (Ralph Hone notes that she did not suffer a complete breakdown as a result of her illness, but it was apparently serious enough to disrupt her schooling.)[8] Despite this physical and emotional disaster, the inner strength of the young woman bore her through the crisis. She won a Gilchrist scholarship to Somerville College and was off to Oxford at last.

For Dorothy L. Sayers, Oxford had a very special meaning. The ancient town with its rivers and narrow streets, its shops and clustered buildings, its towers and libraries, its gowned inhabitants of varied ages and dispositions was in both a literal and a figurative way her first home. Here she had been born, here she had had her first experience of music and learning. In *Gaudy Night*, her Oxford novel, she pictures the cathedral where her father had been the headmaster of the choir school and describes the stately service there, revealing the sense of peace in the dignified and orderly ritual of the Church of England—this time mercifully free of the more gross evidences of the folk. When in need of a soothing influence, her heroine, Harriet Vane, drops by the cathedral to hear services, lingering after the service while the nave empties and the organist finishes the voluntary.[9]

She joined the Bach Choir, and enjoyed singing the music in her rich alto voice. She also seems to have been enormously fond of the choir director, Dr. Hugh Allen. Later, she was to draw much of her imagery from music, having learned to love the music for its own sake, for the beauty of its design, for the mood it brought to her, and for its application to human relationships.

But Oxford was more to the eighteen-year-old student than memories of her father and her childhood. It was the home for her adolescent discovery of self as a woman and a scholar. No woman coming to Oxford could avoid the confrontation with its dominant masculinity. She appeared at Somerville near the end of a great feminist movement. For over forty years women had been seeking to break the sex barrier at Oxford. They had by degrees come to marry the hitherto celibate (or at least bachelor) scholars, then to sit for examinations, then to establish colleges and attend lectures with the men, and finally to compete on the same qualifying examinations. They were still not granted degrees or admitted to some of the professions, but they stood on the verge of those changes as well. Women studying for traditionally male vocations were not allowed to practice them (women studying law, for example, were excluded from the bar), and this forced them to become more vigorous feminists than those in languages, where they did not stand in direct competition with the men. (So long as Sayers was likely to spend her life teaching at a girls' school, she was no particular threat to the men.)

But in the middle of her Oxford years, the men disappeared. War emptied Oxford of almost all male students and professors and drove the women from their residence halls. They lived in lodgings in town while the college was given over to an infirmary. War was to isolate the growing woman once again and delay the time when she would know friendship with or love of men. It also led her into a "woman-ridden" existence full of other problems.

Two of her novels discuss the difficulties of women without men: *Unnatural Death* and *Gaudy Night*. Especially in the latter novel, she discusses, from the vantage point of a mature and far more worldly woman, the strengths and limitations of the life of the woman scholar isolated from men. Her college is, unfortunately, called Shrewsbury, thereby imaging the shrewishness of its inmates. The study apparently offended her old school, though the different characters are presented as types rather than as individual portraits. Sayers had little inclination to join other women in a feminist movement, and little bitterness about "womanly" women—so long as they did not inflict their will on others. The most sinister figure in *Gaudy Night* is an "old-fashioned woman," a "loving mother," who would lie, rob, or murder for her husband and children and call the actions "virtue." She would also deny her children their own proper vocations, insisting that the one who prefers to work on motorcycles must instead be a homemaker. Since Dorothy L. Sayers herself became a motorcycle enthusiast shortly after college, the taste for machines is presented as clearly laudable. The traditional woman insists that a girl must not work in a garage: it is man's work, and she is taking work away from a man; and she will get ugly and dirty and will never attract a husband. Little Beatrice (the ironic name given this "errant" child in *Gaudy Night*) will grow up to be frustrated and conformist, a victim of perverse love. Another Beatrice, Dante's, will later appear to Sayers as no such projection of Victorian Pre-Raphaelite ideals, but as a complex and real woman. The fully mature Sayers was to use her as her final symbol of the role of woman and of love. As she said, the end of her life was there in the beginning.

For Dorothy L. Sayers herself, raised by loving, sensitive, and enlightened parents, the notion of determining a vocation for another person made no sense. This was the period of her life when she was on the brink of deciding her own way, and her father seems to have avoided the role of Evangelist, pointing out the gate to the young pilgrim. He let her find it for herself and offered refuge when she came back from false starts and painful tumbles. If her father had any ambition for her, it probably was that she should become a scholar and finally an Oxford don.

The temptation to give her life over to scholarship seems to have recurred with regularity all through her life, but the choice was her own. Sayers' character Cattermole in *Gaudy Night* is just the opposite—she is *never* tempted to scholarship, is lost at Oxford, and finds herself in one scrape after another. When finally quizzed on her unhappiness, she admits that she would rather be a cook than a historian but has been forced to her education by upward-striving parents. Her mother, as perverse in her own way as little Beatrice's, is " 'one of those people who work to get things open to women.' "[10] Sayers' point is simple: there is no proper place or proper work except one's own—that which is individually fitted to the needs and talents of the person. A young woman should be at Oxford if she wants to study Aristotle. A young man should avoid it like the plague if he does not want to study Aristotle or anything else. There is no such thing as a "woman's sphere," or a "man's."

One must find one's vocation—the work one is meant to do—if one is to find happiness. This theme is enormously important to Sayers, and it was at Oxford that she was most clearly presented with the choices available for her. Education is preparation for work: " 'If you learn how to tackle one subject—any subject—you've learnt how to tackle all subjects.' "[11] But for woman the end of formal education is often a fork in the road. One road leads still further into the groves of academe; another leads into practical and rocky territory where new skills are needed; and another into what seemed to Sayers a dead end: the rose-covered cottage of matrimony. The paths need not be so clearly separated, but for women they often have been. Women are confronted with a choice of career or marriage that would be laughable if applied to a man.

The women at Shrewsbury (the fictionalized version of Somerville) who elected the academic path are varied in a number of ways. But only one is married, and she finds herself the victim of conflicting loyalties. A sick child can take her away from work at a crucial moment, leading the other women to quarrel with her priorities. She is finally hounded out of her job, not by the men, but by the women, who do not share her problems. The woman stands in agony between two concepts, the old loyalty to family and the new one to vocation. If she makes her priorities human ones (as any decent man would also do under similar circumstances), she reveals herself to be an unreconstructed hausfrau. The burden is sufficient to upset, embarrass, and finally discourage her.

The other scholars have a range of responses to their lives of celibate intellectualism. Some have chosen virginity; some have had it thrust upon them. Miss Hillyard, a vocal and abusive feminist, rejoices in her independence, despises men, and reacts with perverse jealousy when others enjoy the company and affection of men. Her term break is spent with a married sister who is having a baby, and she is delighted to return to the simple existence of Oxford. For her it is clear that her scholarly work is always paramount.

Miss de Vine has, by contrast, made the cool and rational choice of vocation. She had once been engaged, but had found that she was a thoughtless lover because her heart was not in the relationship, and so broke it off. Having almost no interest in human relations, she observes others, comments dispassionately, and feels little. Her ability to place scholarship above human relations makes her a brilliant historian, unfit for most close human contact.

Others in the college also seem to have chosen their careers with wisdom. Miss Lydgate, another excellent scholar, has an open and gracious heart, but no real interest in much of life outside of her narrow study of English prosody. Like Miss de Vine, she considers no personalities when she attacks falsehood. In her mental life, there are no divided loyalties.

The Dean also appears happy in her work and more congenial, witty, and human in personal relations, therefore more suited to administration and amelioration of conflict. Certain motherly qualities find outlet in mothering the scholars in her care.

A common denominator of these women is their separation from the men: the administrators, secretaries, scouts, and scholars, with their different family backgrounds and different interests—all are living apart from men. Only Harriet D. Vane, the mystery writer, brings men into the college with her and goes out to meet them. She notes that this "tower set on a hill" might easily become the home of "soured virginity." The scholars seem to look at life with a "single eye"—a limited and exclusive vision. But she learns that they, like all people, must reconcile heart and brain. For this, they need a "stereoscopic vision."[12] By the end of the story, she is less convinced that virginity has warped these women or made them unhappy; but it is clear that the cloistered life is not her choice. She is too hungry for the world.

By all reports, Dorothy Sayers did enjoy herself enormously at Oxford as an undergraduate. Active in music, dramatics, in college life, she was primarily a scholar, eager to prove herself to those she admired. Her relationships with faculty were long lasting. Not only did she return for visits, but she sent books to favorite teachers and kept up a correspondence with them. Her early effort at translating *Roland*, which brought forth admiring words from Mildred Pope, was to stay in her heart for years. She was proud of taking a first in languages, and she never lost her love of good scholarship.

Sir Basil Blackwell characterized her in her college days as "gallant and gay."[13] Her ebullient laughter bubbled up easily. She was as willing to aim her barbed wit at herself as at another. And she learned that the best cure for tragedy is comedy, calling laughter the "paraclete of pain."[14] In one of her early poems, she notes that laughter bubbles up from within her, driving away the pain. This remarkable humor was to explain much of her resilience in life. If she could not win the love of the choirmaster, she could parody her crush on him in a school play she wrote for graduation (or "going down"). And if she could not be beautiful, she could wear a great wig with a black bow, a purple gown, parrot earrings, and smoke a cigar. Perhaps the comic choices were for her, as they were for the sensitive Lord Peter, a protective mask. But they were also fun, and she was independent enough to do whatever she enjoyed doing.

We know that Sayers found pleasure in the companionship of intelligent women, and discovered among the students at Oxford several lifetime friends. A group formed, gathered together because of common interests, and called themselves, at Sayers' suggestion, the "Mutual Admiration Society"—because, she said, if they didn't, the rest of Somerville would. They continued meeting for the rest of their lives, sharing ideas and occasionally collaborating on writing. Muriel St. Clare Byrne, Charis Barnett, and Marjorie Barber—along with a number of others—were members of this group and formed an important and continuing part of Sayers' life.[15]

With the combination of her increasingly individual appearance and practices and the absence of young men from her life (she says she really never knew a young man her own age until she was twenty-five), she was not even tempted by the tender trap of matrimony. Her experience when she returned years later for her own reunion, or "Gaudy Night," like Harriet's, was to see the enormous waste of good minds in matrimony: "All that brilliance, all that trained intelligence, harnessed to a load that any uneducated country girl could have drawn, and drawn far better."[16] She rarely found the woman who married young and abandoned her mental pursuits to be as interesting or as happy as one who had seen more of life. Her great ideal is the marriage with a man who can allow the woman's individual development, blending her vocation with his own so that both may grow. She did not see any comfortable way of blending child-rearing with her notion of meaningful work, suspecting the career woman would need domestic help or family to provide for youngsters.

For her, Oxford was the city of peace, the still center in a whirling world, the home of "Pax Academia to a world terrified with unrest." Certainly to be in the stillness of Oxford in the middle of World War I would accentuate the enduring values of education, of culture over anarchy. As she herself said, this is the place where one is admonished to be true to one's calling, no matter what follies one might commit otherwise. This is the way of "spiritual peace. How could one feel fettered, being the freeman of so great a city?"[17]

Oxford always meant a great deal to Dorothy L. Sayers, as the home of intellectual achievement, of honored work, of quiet pursuit of truth. " 'Whatever I may have done since,' " says her Harriet, " 'this remains. Scholar; Master of Arts; Domina; Senior Member of this University.' " It is " 'a place achieved, inalienable, worthy of reverence.' "[18] For Dorothy L. Sayers, receiving simultaneously her B.A., M.A., and B.C.L. degrees, it was a great experience. At this largest assembly of graduates Oxford had ever seen, including 4181 men and 549 women, the first fully qualified women graduates in the history of the university stood before the vice-chancellor. Cheers broke out spontaneously. Dorothy Sayers never forgot that moment—what it symbolized in the life of the intellect, and what its delay said about the life of womankind.[19]

The lures of the city were undeniable, but on "going down," she wrote, "go hence and seek your own renown."[20] The gray-walled serenity of Oxford had been her first, but it was not her final, or her spiritual home. Her pilgrim soul demanded the dust and struggle of the warfaring world, not the cloistered security of this "enchanted town." Her way was to lead to Hull, to France, to Oxford again, and finally to Vanity Fair—London town.

II. Vanity Fair

All liberal arts graduates without teaching interests and without independent wealth are faced with the problem of finding jobs relevant to their education. In the "real world" (i. e., the world of money and food and housing), of what use are they? For the Christian, the need for the right work, not just a profitable job, is absolutely essential; Sayers thought that the discovery and practice of proper work is central to the happiness of every person.

Dorothy L. Sayers tried and rejected the traditional role of schoolmistress—the safe path for unmarried and unmonied rectors' daughters. Her students in the girls' schools where she briefly taught languages thought her an excellent and exuberant teacher, attractive and fun. She threw herself into the work, encouraging students to write poetry in French, directing plays, and joining in the school life. But to a mind hungry for scholarly and worldly knowledge as well as wide experience, the staid residence among adolescent girls, and the repetition of the old studies would be stultifying. She hungered for a larger life than the small salary and tight schedule of the resident schoolmarm could provide.

She next considered the craft she had learned in her studies of literature and language: she knew how to use words. First, drawn briefly back to Oxford, she played with the editing and publishing of other people's words. She worked at Blackwell's, a publisher in the center of her beloved town, and lived nearby. But again, this was clearly not her vocation. It allowed no outlet for her creativity and imagination, and the pay was too meager to allow travel, or even subsistence. Her father supplemented her paltry earnings with a regular stipend. This too seemed an unnecessary prolongation of adolescence. However, Blackwell's was useful to Sayers in providing professional experience and the opportunity to see her works in print.

In a series of small, limited editions, this publisher encouraged her and other budding young poets by printing some of their talented juvenilia. Hers were poems in the metaphysical mode for the most part, though some were pseudo-medieval ballad and lyric forms, and one was a satiric verse drama. The ideas and images of these early collections, *Op. I* and *Catholic Tales and Christian Songs,* foreshadow her mature patterns. She pictures Christ as the "bonny outlaw," and attacks the tidy and conformist world that would bind Christ and crucify him. If she had, as Hitchman reports, flirted with agnosticism earlier, she had abandoned the flirtation by the time she wrote this poetry. In addition to expressing an emotional and fundamental faith, the poems show her laughing at herself, waxing lyrical, enjoying erudite allusions, and playing easily with contemporary ideas.

The poems, some of which appeared in the same series as ones by her young contemporary at Oxford, Aldous Huxley, demonstrate taste and ability. But they were not the sort of thing that was destined to bring the poor clergyman's daughter fame or fortune. Yeats, Eliot, Pound, and others dominated the poetic scene. The mood of the postwar era demanded the broken poetry of disillusionment, not the modest and mannered struggles of adolescent girls. She never really thought of herself as more than a second-rate talent in poetry. When she confessed this some years later to her friend Dr. Barbara Reynolds, the young scholar responded that she considered Sayers a very good poet indeed. The startled Sayers demanded, "Why didn't you tell me that before?" Sayers always longed to be a poet and loved other people's poetry—especially the seventeenth-century poets'. She used poetry lavishly in her books, imitated it, and translated a good bit of it. But her reluctance to bare her soul and give vent to her feelings in print prevented her from developing the confessional or neo-Romantic styles that appeal to the modern. The path to renown and to comfortable income lay not in writing or in editing lyric poetry. (It is ironic that her last financial and artistic success was a verse translation.) She was, in fact, convinced that the reading public was more interested in "penny dreadfuls," the cheap thrillers that were bought by the millions. She started reading these while enjoying the ambience of Oxford.

Living in a small house in a back street near Blackwell's, she came to enjoy a different Oxford from the one she had known as a student. Now men were returning to the town, among them C. S. Lewis (whom she did not meet until some years later). She found she especially enjoyed the company of a young war veteran named Eric Whelpton. He recalls that of the forty-six young men in his house at Oxford, twenty-eight had been killed in the war and others were badly crippled. He returned tired and ill and seeking a change from the horrors of war. Dorothy Sayers brought him good companionship and good talk. Recalling that she was "far from beautiful," he nonetheless found her lively and intelligent. They met two or three times a week, usually in the company of other people. His elegant clothing and financial resources contrasted strangely with her drab garb and poverty—though no one could say she was ever really drab. Reports of the period indicate she occasionally smoked a cigar in the daring postbellum mode of sophistication. Whelpton credits his friend Sayers with educating him, helping him to return to the world of books and ideas after four years of war. He could not understand her taste for cheap novels, especially murder mysteries, which he disapproved of, but he was delighted at her wide reading in the English classics.

When he left Oxford, he took a position with the École des Roches in Normandy, and later asked that Dorothy Sayers come to join him as his assistant. She left her job at Blackwell's and (with her parents' permission) joined him, probably hoping that their affection would deepen into love. They worked together for a year, spending twenty to thirty hours a week by themselves. But he insists that their relationship was never physical. It was purely intellectual on his side, he insists (in the tone of a well-bred gentleman), and passionate on hers (he says). Apparently, he was in love with another woman, using her as a shield against his young assistant's passion. "Our friendship," he recalled at the age of 88, "was noble and dignified and a source of inspiration to me."[1]

It was clearly a source of inspiration for Dorothy Sayers as well. France thereafter became her symbol for healthy views on love and sex. This was not her first or last trip to this country she had learned to love first through its language, but it was undoubtedly the most emotionally charged visit. Dorothy Sayers was enough of a scholar in medieval romance to appreciate the long and rich tradition of love literature developed in this country. She came to France at the peak of her youthful romanticism, eager for adventure. She spent her time in the company of a dapper and disillusioned young war veteran with a doomed passion for a mysterious lady who, in his romantic words, "died soon after." And she was busy reading cheap, sensational novels in her spare time. It is no wonder, given this conjunction of elements, that she was to conclude that French attitudes toward sex and romance are far healthier and more fun than English. Whenever Lord Peter, who dresses in clothes reminiscent of Eric Whelpton's, speaks of love, he breaks spontaneously into French—the proper language for improper passion.

At the end of her Gallic year, Dorothy Sayers asked Whelpton to join her in writing detective novels, but he refused on the grounds that he disliked them and "the public would not fall for anything so sordid." They parted soon after, writing to one another occasionally, but seldom meeting thereafter.

She returned to England, received her long-awaited degree, and looked around again for a job. She took a temporary job at the Girls' High School at Clapham, and then finally got her chance for adventure.

Her chance for a new life—and eventually for literary success—came with a job offer from Benson's Advertising Agency in London. In the great upsurge of advertising which started early in the twentieth century, Benson's realized the need for a woman on the staff, supposedly to provide ideas that would appeal to women. Dorothy Sayers replaced the first woman to work as "ideas man and copywriter" for the firm. Although she considered it a temporary job, she stayed for nine years.

London, where she found a small flat in Bloomsbury, was a great contrast to the university or market towns she knew so well. A great bustling commercial and artistic center, it was bursting with life of every description. The parson's daughter saw it as a place of unlimited opportunity. In the village, people had established identities and roles, acting them out like "chessmen upon their allotted squares," but in the city—especially in London—"anybody, at any moment, might do or become anything."[2] Such challenging freedom to choose one's identity and activity was inebriating to the twenty-eight-year-old woman.

Her flat on Great James Street was convenient to work and to the activities that attracted her in this busy town. She settled eagerly into the life of the career woman—a heady adventure for a young woman even today, but especially so in the early years of our century when such chances were so rare. The experience of being away from home and friends, of being on one's own, self-reliant in an especially frightening way, even now thrills the young adult, but Sayers must have felt the additional excitement of the pioneer. The "new women" or "Bloomsbury women" or "Chelsea women," as they are variously called, were shocking to the post-Victorian world. They were often flamboyant, iconoclastic, and independent career women who rejected the Victorian rules of decorum and domesticity for a new freedom. They became artists, doctors, lawyers; they experimented with ideas and alcohol and sex; they smoked in public and seemed incredibly daring and decadent to the more traditional and respectable British citizens. Sayers' experiences in France appear to have liberated her from parsonage morality and she seems to have relished her cigarettes and her freedom.

She bought a motorcycle so she could visit home—now Christchurch—whenever she liked. And she did return home to write her books and to share her troubles. Meanwhile, she looked around her. The city was full of art circles, political groups, clubs, and ideas. Although she lived in Bloomsbury at the same time the famous Bloomsbury group gathered at the home of Virginia and Leonard Woolf, she was not a part of their elegant aesthetic circle. The artists she describes were more bohemian—the sculptors, painters, and writers who occasionally did and more commonly did not earn enough from their art to eke out an existence. She describes with wit and verve their arguments about new art movements and about the vivid personalities of the day. She laughs at the "Book of the Moment Club" and the worship of the great god Whirl. She describes the crowded Soviet Club, the wild drinking parties, the free sex life, the intense conversations in smoky rooms about Freud and glands and Marx. She catches the vitality and confusion of an exciting time. It is clear that the variegated life of London charmed her and appalled her.

The advertising business itself is vividly and realistically described in one of the last Lord Peter novels, *Murder Must Advertise.* Miss Hitchman and others have testified that the book is an excellent portrayal of the hectic and hilarious world of the burgeoning advertising industry, with its search for slogans, race with deadlines, love of gimmicks, and pandering to poor taste. From the inside, it must have been interesting; for the intelligent and educated people who develop the advertising campaigns must be quick, flexible, aggressive, shrewd, and imaginative. They must understand the dreams of the public, the limitations of taste, the latent appetites, and the means to stimulate a demand for luxury or health or beauty.

As Sayers notes, they aimed their campaigns, not at the wealthy, who can and do buy what they want when they want, but at the middle and poorer classes, who ache for "a luxury beyond their reach and for a leisure for ever denied them." These eager victims are "bullied or wheedled into spending their few hardly won shillings on whatever might give them, if only for a moment, a leisured and luxurious illusion."[3] Certainly the perpetrators of this phantasmagoria, if they manipulate others as they are paid to do, must be either enormously cynical or morally neutral.

Sayers' own role as spokesperson for the "woman's angle" must have been comic at best. She, like her Miss Meteyard in the novel, probably found she could write about practically anything but women's goods. Sayers' most famous campaign was for mustard, a product without sexual implications. Certain men in the office, not the least bit effiminate, "could handle corsets and face-cream with a peculiar plaintive charm" that made them indispensable for the female market.[4] Sayers laughs at the notion that all women think alike—and that all men do—and that therefore any woman would naturally write copy about corsets better than any man. In *Are Women Human?* she suggests that when we wonder whether a woman could do a job better than a man, we should consider which man, which woman, and which job.

Some men and some women cannot write appealingly about anything, and some men know a good bit more about clothing or cosmetics than some women. (Sayers herself rarely used any cosmetics other than powder.) "What is unreasonable and irritating is to assume that *all* one's tastes and preferences have to be conditioned by the class to which one belongs."[5]

For the time being, the job proved interesting and modestly profitable. Copywriters, as she describes them in *Murder Must Advertise,* are frequently both affable and witty. The life as she knew it combined a freedom of sorts, creativity, and good company. The firm was considerate—though not generous—in its relations to its workers, keeping them content with their genteel poverty.

But she also cites the inherent problems that made copywriting a job for her survival, not a vocation for fulfillment. The advertiser's job is to sell, not to judge. The client must be pleased and the public must be moved if the copywriter is to keep the job. Pleasing seldom involves truth; selling rarely develops balanced thinking. The profession, she says in her novel, has as its essence telling plausible lies for money.[6] Legalism rather than morality dominates word choices. The word "pure," for example, has a legal meaning that could involve the client in litigation; the words "highest quality" are without legal meaning and, though equally false, a better choice.

Dorothy L. Sayers found that her established literary, philosophic, and religious scruples challenged her at every step to repudiate the work she was doing. Her sense of vocation—a calling by God himself to do one's own proper work—was daily violated by the work she was actually doing. She could not, like others around her, casually separate her work from her life, becoming a scrupulously moral person in private life and an amoral person in public. She could assuage her conscience only by insisting that she was doing the work well and that she had to earn her own living by some means. She was good at the work, found real relish in her "Mustard Club" campaign, and occasionally felt tempted to dabble in advertising thoughout her life, partly because it was lucrative, and partly because she was good at it. Later she was to work on propaganda for the government, using her craft for her country in wartime.

She also wondered about the giddy cycle of supply and demand creating a "hell's-dance of spending and saving." If all the advertising in the world were suddenly to cease, all the admonitions to buy more oats, drink more beer, pop more pills, take better care of your complexion, your digestion, your baby, and your husband were to stop for a moment, what would happen? "Would people still go on buying more soap, eating more apples, giving their children more vitamins and roughage?"[7] She perceived the root sin to be gluttony and accused the advertising industry of flattering and frightening people "out of a reasonable contentment into a greedy hankering after goods which they do not really need."[8] She saw her country to be in real peril when it depended on a system that kept up this dreadful "whirligig of industrial finance based on gluttonous consumption." This "overmuch stuffing of ourselves is the sin that has delivered us over into the power of the machine."[9]

For Dorothy L. Sayers the advertising world really does lie at the center of Vanity Fair. Hawking false values, pandering to our basest qualities, perverting our judgment, disguising tawdry goods for valuable, it creates illusion and fosters moral depravity. The constant focus on our material nature and on the world's vanities debases both the victim and the perpetrator. "'Fear not him that killeth,'" quotes the Christian apologist Parker, in viewing this world, "'but him that hath power to cast into hell.'"[10]

The hell into which Sayers feared that she would be cast was the vacuous world of the Trimmers, those who will make no choices. Eventually, if we judge by the faintly autobiographical character of Miss Meteyard in *Murder Must Advertise*, the ethical perversity of this work drains one of the ability to judge. Though she knows of adultery, blackmail, and murder, she is reluctant to interfere or comment. Moral neutrality is the natural result of the dichotomized mind, constantly shirking responsibility for moral judgment in any sphere. Sayers was discovering that, if one has no respect for the work one is doing, one also soon loses any respect for oneself as a person.

The city panders to more tastes more cynically than the small town does. The city's shops full of charming extravagances coax the coins from the purse. The restaurants and bakeshops with their luscious aromas and signs lure the passer to gluttony. The plays and books and newspapers announce multiple truths, usually masking multiple lies.

And the speakers in Hyde Park or the social clubs proclaim their angle of vision as the only valid one. In an anonymous world, no one need feel especially responsible for words or acts, or worry about the consequences in the frivolous or sinister behavior of others. The con artist shrewd enough and quick enough can take all the profits and leave the payment and the cleanup for others.

The moral corruptions of this Tower of Babel are matched by the aesthetic ones. Taste deteriorates as the artist lies and the audience reacts viscerally, to the exclusion of the intellect. The debasement of language is a real evil to one who believes in communication, in the value of words, and in beauty. In fact, George Orwell also pointed out a few years later that verbal distortion is itself a threat to freedom. Sayers was quick to note that every item for sale was "unique" or "fantastic" or the "greatest," the "best," the "newest." Moderation in language seldom sells merchandise or books. Linguistic overkill has become a staple in the modern world.

As an implied comment, when she wrote her advertising novel, Sayers placed this City of Dreadful Day against another city—the City of Dreadful Night—a world of dope-peddling and crime. The genial colleagues in the advertising office mirror the underworld as they lie, cheat, and murder. The "innocence" of this daylight world is matched by the guilty shadows of its sinsiter double; both are full of corruption, both sell false dreams for a tidy profit.

But Dorothy Sayers stayed with Benson's, learning her craft and discovering more about British taste than she ever dreamed possible. She later said that, in her writing, she decided what people wanted, and then what she would let them have. She made the most of her experience, enjoyed the companionship, read stacks of mystery stories, developed friendships among other artists, and learned a great deal about life outside the rectory and the college. It was typical of her that she consistently accepted reality with a spirit of adventure, with a good nature, and with a clear judgment, and then set about to do the necessary work with vigor. But she just as characteristically kept her eye on the path she knew to be her own, and the means by which to climb back onto the King's Highway.

She had elected, though not consciously, to be a saint in the world, not in the cloister. She saw herself not as St. Theresa, but as Faust.

Confronting the world, the flesh, and the devil, she was determined to understand and to experience as much as she could. The unquestioning morality of the village rectory and the unswerving taste of the university community gave her the necessary foundations from which to judge her world. But she was not content to watch life without touching it, to cultivate lofty detachment without personal involvement. The dangers were obvious: she stood in peril of losing her intellectual and moral purity in the eyes of the world, and of losing her heart and soul in the eyes of the church. The risk proved both exciting and painful.

Her first move was to dip into popular fiction, apparently disregarding the years of careful classical preparation. She risked her reputation as a scholar and a woman of culture as she apparently exchanged the Oxford mortarboard for a foolscap. For years she had been reading every possible form of crime, detective, and mystery tale—the cheap ones, the antique ones, and the intellectual ones. Over the years, she had read Arthur Conan Doyle, Edgar Wallace, G. K. Chesterton, Wilkie Collins, E. C. Bentley, and dozens of others. Her delight in the genre, her pleasure with puzzles, and her interest in fame led her to believe that this was her path to success. She could break into the literary field by writing stories of detection, especially if she made them witty and shrewdly contrived.

Of all her mystery figures, the character most obviously taken from her experience at Benson's—apart from those in *Murder Must Advertise*—is Montague Egg. This precise, attractive, and practical young salesman of fine spirits (i. e., expensive wine) appears in numerous short stories. Having memorized the sententious maxims of the *Salesman's Handbook*, he goes his quiet and dignified way from client to client and from crime to crime, using the manual's pithy advice to sum up his findings and his methods. For example, one story ends with this aphorism from his favorite book:

> *To Serve the Public is the aim*
> *Of every salesman worth the name.*[11]

Edgar Guest could hardly have written a worse verse.

The tongue-in-cheek presentation of the perfect salesman is a real delight. His quick observation (an essential for sizing up customers and catering to their needs) is coupled with a poker face (for no salesman can allow the customer to notice his displeasure or disdain). He easily spots crimes and solves them, identifies malefactors, and hands them over to the police (if he is called upon to intervene) with bland indifference to the moral values involved.

But Sayers' supreme creation, Lord Peter Wimsey, is barely tempted by sales at all. He does enjoy his brief masquerade as a copywriter at Pym's (Benson's), but he is disgusted with the rationale and results of advertising. As his trapped creator started sketching him on paper, she must have found him a congenial companion and a distinct relief from her own limitations. He could share her tastes (for scholarship and beauty and wit) and could, in addition, indulge them. With his wealth, he could purchase the rare manuscripts, savor the fine wines, attend the concerts, and surround himself with beauty. Though he was not much better looking than she—and about the same age—he could laugh at his parrot nose and receding forehead. His slight stature and frivolous ways make him appear "unmanly," but his wealth and wit redeem him in the face of his critics. A man with ugly features can laugh at them and prove his worth in other ways. For many years, Lord Peter understandably was her favorite character. He rescued her from her anger with her work, entertained her with his unlimited potential for adventure, helped her puzzle out her problems, and finally saved her from a lifetime of improper work. It is no wonder that she finally came to see him as slightly Christlike.

Murder Must Advertise was a late Lord Peter novel. He had first appeared in *Whose Body?* and then in a series of detective stories which gradually brought Sayers an enthusiastic public and a comfortable income. Typically, she preferred to write about events in her life after she had time to contemplate them. She wrote about advertising after leaving Benson's, about the fen country and her family after her parents' deaths, and about Oxford long after her graduation and shortly after a return visit for a Gaudy Night speech. Therefore, the chronology of her life does not neatly match the subject matter of her books.

Lord Peter was a compound of detectives Sayers had met in studies of fiction (Philip Trent, Sherlock Holmes, and others); of men she had known (Eric Whelpton and others noted by Alzina Stone Dale[12] and discussed in various places by Dr. Barbara Reynolds, Janet Hitchman, and Ralph Hone); of her own personality and of her vivid imagination.

87411
FERNALD LIBRARY
COLBY-SAWYER COLLEGE
NEW LONDON, N.H. 03257

He is, like God's creation, far more than the sum of his parts. A living, growing, maturing creature, he was also, like the postlapsarian Adam, doomed to die by his very insistence on his own human freedom.

Dorothy L. Sayers must have had fun creating and enlarging on this hero, whom she apparently planned from the beginning as the hero of a series of stories. She could give him her facility in modern and classical languages, her love of the French and their notions about the sexes, her eclectic taste in literature, her joy in music, her respect for decorum and authority and precision. But she could also give him the many things denied her—wealth, position, a priceless butler, exquisite taste in clothes and foods, impressive social contacts, sophisticated continental sexual experience, elegant manners, and, of course, manhood. Thus he could dabble where others must drudge. He never need compromise his ideals for popularity or money.

He appeals to women and clearly enjoys them. "Uncle Pandarus," the character Paul Austin Delagardie, explains his own role in Peter's sex education by explaining elliptically about introducing the young man to the French arts of love. Wimsey has no British reticence about sex and says that the only sin against passion is to lie down without joy. There must be joy and a regard for the other. Although kind to unattractive women and fatherly in his advice to them, he never takes advantage of women or confuses love with passion. He has been disappointed in love and understands the disappointment felt by others. His interest is usually whetted by a clever woman with warmth and forthrightness. Unlike most heroes of adventure stories, he has no interest in dominating another human being.

Over a number of books we learn a good bit about Lord Peter, his family, and his friends. We see various of the Wimsey residences, including the palatial family estate at Denver, and the country home at Riddlesdale; and we meet his pompous nephew, his intense sister, and his magnificent mother.

We eventually learn about the family arms: sable, three mice courant argent; crest, a domestic cat crouched as to spring, proper; motto "As My Whimsy Takes Me." We find he took a first at Oxford in history, is still remembered as Wimsey of Balliol because of his spectacular plays in cricket, can drive faster, play the piano and the harpsichord more perfectly, and speak more wittily than any man most of us have ever known. He is famous for his palate as a wine taster, can perform card tricks, punt a boat, swim, dance, and so on. No matter what the occasion, he either knows someone to do the job or can do it himself, with a flourish. It is no wonder that Harriet Vane, seeing him elevated on horseback, called him "god-like."

He served in World War I in the army in France, where his monocle earned him the nickname of "Old Winderpane" from his devoted subordinates. He still remembers by name those who served with him. During an enemy attack, he was buried alive for some time; after his rescue he suffered from a nervous breakdown, and still has occasional nervous seizures when he is disturbed. His faithful servant Bunter, who served with him as his sergeant, shared that experience with him and came to him in his darkest days to nurse him back to health. Bunter selects his clothes, orders his household, helps to investigate and photograph crimes, and generally serves as mother, wife, and friend until Harriet comes along to share some of the burden.

In most of the early stories, Lord Peter is a comic figure, as pretentious as an Oscar Wilde man-about-town, as irreverent as a Noel Coward *bon vivant.* He seems far too frivolous to care about the human tragedy that is invariably antecedent to his entrance into the murder investigation, and takes an amoral interest in the puzzle of detection. Here we see, briefly, a person who views a body as comic, a murder as a conundrum, and detection as a fox hunt. Unlike Montague Egg, Lord Peter quickly changes into a moral and deeply emotional human being. But it is clear that he was originally conceived as a suitable hero for a modern mock-epic—or perhaps more correctly, for a travesty in which human pain is trivialized by the detached intellect.

Since Lord Peter is so divorced from the common activities of the average person, he needs associates beyond the loyal and incredible Bunter to bring him into touch with the world of bourgeois melodrama where the murders often occur. For this, he draws into his sphere Miss Climpson, an elderly spinster of impressive intellectual resources, who helps in detection by indulging in apparently mindless gossip. Her veneer of silly gabbiness hides a shrewd common sense that can manipulate a conversation and extract pertinent information from a plethora of irrelevance. Artistically and philosophically she is useful in the novels as a contrast to Lord Peter: her middle-class spinster life sets off his advantages, and her deeply held—and strongly voiced—religious convictions underscore his reticence.

And, inevitably, because he needs the authority and information-gathering services of the established law-enforcement agencies, he has as his best friend a police officer—Chief Inspector Charles Parker (originally only Inspector Parker). He too, like Miss Climpson, provides an explicitly Christian commentary on the activities of the novel. He is a more orderly person than Lord Peter, a more plodding methodologist, necessarily more concerned with details of procedure and evidence.

Gradually, over a period of time, Sayers builds a country setting and a city setting for Peter and his friends. The same people appear in one novel after another, with enlargement and occasional surprise. Though not as richly symbolic and tragically powerful as Faulker's Yoknapawtapha County, Sayers' little world carries much of the same solidity and scope. As Dr. Trevor H. Hall has so thoroughly demonstrated in his chronology of the Lord Peter stories,

> Dorothy L. Sayers, unlike Conan Doyle, kept to a systematic, rigorous and almost totally consistent chronology, extending over eleven novels, 21 short stories and an eleven-part weekly series in a periodical, and covering, from first to last, some twenty years of narrative. In so doing she retained control of her material throughout, giving it a coherence and shapeliness rarely achieved in a work of such length and so many parts.[13]

Sayers is almost always aware of the year, the season, the day of the week (even the phase of the moon), as well as the place, the people, and their various linguistic and historical traditions. Her novels, for all their activity, are firmly rooted in immediate reality. She is following Coleridge's formula for Romanticism, seeking to bring reality to wild adventure by giving it a local habitation and a name. Like Coleridge, she drew heavily on her well-stocked mind, full of trivia and rich understanding from vast and often undisciplined reading. Later, when she read in *The Road to Xanadu* John Livingston Lowes' description of Coleridge's imaginative process, she was delighted to discover the revelance to her own. As Dr. Reynolds has often noted, if we want to understand Dorothy L. Sayers completely, we must look not so much to her life as to her reading; we must read what she read.

Certainly her long reading in the genre of detective fiction came to her service. She especially admired Wilkie Collins', *The Moonstone* and E. C. Bentley's *Trent's Last Case.* She described her thrill at the latter in almost mystic terms: years after reading it she still recalled, in a conversation with Dr. Reynolds, the "liberating and inspiring influence" it had on her.

> The old stock characters were gone, and in their place were real people, Trent the journalist, Marlowe, Bunner, old Mr. Cupples, and, still more astonishing, Mrs. Manderson the heroine—all breathing and moving with abounding vitality. . . . There was the amazingly [sic], the enthralling novelty. . . . And even the love-story, so often a weak disaster, is in this masterly book, made moving, credible and integral to the plot.[14]

Dr. Reynolds has thoroughly documented Sayers' debt to Bentley; others have found clear parallels to Sherlock Holmes, Bertie Wooster, and Sir Charles Grandison. A case can even be made for Tristram Shandy. Sayers delights in planting clues in her books about her sources, parodying some of her predecessors and laughing at their more obvious techniques and flaws. For example, she has Lord Peter mock the outrageous deductions Holmes makes from the slightest shard of evidence, and comments on the remarkable fact that his dear Watson could follow his friend for twenty years without ever developing the least notion of his methods. It is hard to believe anyone could be that obtuse. By way of contrast, Lord Peter surrounds himself with people who are resourceful and bright and can help him with his search for facts and links.

In her address entitled "The Craft of Detective Fiction,"[15] Dorothy Sayers notes the requirements for the amateur detective in successful fiction: the chance to be consulted about crimes, the freedom to investigate them without worries about working hours and family responsibilities, the ability to apply a wide range of information to cases without undue research or reliance on contacting experts, the physique to "cope with violent criminals," the leisure and wealth to follow clues wherever they lead (chartering planes, hiring associates, etc.), and the youth to allow for maturing over a series of novels. Sensing from the beginning that Lord Peter had a long career ahead of him, she contrived him with great care.

Dorothy Sayers explained that writing detective stories, like writing advertisements, was largely the art of framing believable lies.[16] She was forthright in her explanation of procedures for writing. In the introduction to the three volumes of *The Omnibus of Crime* and in numerous articles, notably "Gaudy Night," she explains with great precision the nature of the form, what it must include and exclude, what choices are necessary, and why she made the selections she did. She notes, for example, that she had from the outset "envisaged for Peter a prolonged and triumphal career, going on through book after book amid the plaudits of adoring multitudes."[17] She set for herself—and later for the London Detection Club—certain rigid standards: the novels must be probable, they must be complete, they must have a basic Aristotelian unity. In logical progression, they must take all the evidence into account and must play fair with the reader in providing all the necessary evidence for deducing the conclusion. They should not be based on a sudden revelation at the conclusion or an improbable confession—no *deus ex machina* was allowed. They must finally account in their solution for the inevitable triad of motive, method, and opportunity. The details of place and activity must be rigorously researched and exact insofar as this is humanly possible. She admitted with a self-deprecating laugh that she had a "howler" in every book, though she was conscientious in her research.

She knew all the possibilities for detective fiction and catalogued them neatly in her invariably methodical way: a confession is weak artistically and must be bolstered by supporting evidence; the device of the "least likely person" may be used only if the secret motive has been hinted earlier in the story; fake evidence is allowable if the flaw is apparent in the presentation; a trick murder method is especially fun because it demands the ingenuity of the community to solve the riddle; and of course the hidden key—usually a puzzle, code, or map—is acceptable if one allows the reader to join in the process of the solution.

Even though one might allow for her taste in the form, her appetite for fame and fortune, and her love of organizing knowledge, her decision to take Lord Peter and his cohorts into fiction still puzzles many. There are, in fact, some natural ties to her own earlier work and some relevancies to her immediate emotional and psychological needs.

Her great love of medieval art forms, especially epic and romance, found an outlet in this modern popular romance form. Just as she had enjoyed imitating the mode of medieval poetry, she found in this debased form the seeds of a folk art that she could enjoy shaping. Dr. Reynolds, a medievalist herself, notes that epic and romance are essential components of Sayers' detective fiction. She uses something of the Arthurian cycle, even more of the matter of France. Several times she alludes to Peter's parallels to Roland and Parker's to Oliver. Hitchman sees in the Bunter-Peter association a squire-knight relation.[18] She uses the pageantry (especially in *Clouds of Witness*), the code of honor, the proper dressing of the hero, the aristocratic status and artificial speech, the central conflict of good and evil.[19]

Her other tastes in literature are also obvious. Her form, as already noted, is basically Aristotelian, but her approach is Shakespearean. Like the old master, she is not embarrassed when she pleases the groundlings as well as the scholars; like him, she is a dealer in sensation and in beauty; like him she employs "the popular appeal to horror, curiosity, and ordinary human feeling which is the very guts and essential necessity of sensation literature."[20]

Sayers' ability to see the vital force in classics was to prove the key to her own success as a writer and as a scholar. She delights in borrowing and adapting older forms and ideas, quoting from works that please her, but she is not afraid to create a new life out of the old one. The contemporary world of which she was so very aware amid the bustle of London has its own romance and sensation. It has its own epic characters, types of national hero. She was never one to believe that older classics were sacrosanct. If they were good, they had life that we need not tiptoe around or bow down and worship. Classics had themselves once dealt with contemporary matters and had pleased a rowdy crew with their bawdy moments, their swashbuckling, and their blood and thunder. We do them disservice to treat them like fragile antiques and we do ourselves a disservice to assume we have nothing new to say. The mystery story may not be one of the greatest types; it is after all very restricted in form. But it is "as capable of its own proper greatness as a sonnet within the restrictions of octave and sestet."[21]

She therefore strove to combine the sense of form she had found in all great literature, the mystery that is the core of the tale of detection, and the good writing that characterizes any valuable literature. Realizing that she was working in the tradition of the English novel, though a very recent form of it, she studied the gothic tales of horror, the tales of the supernatural, of violence, and of detection. For her own taste, the delight of the intellectual unraveling was paramount. Therefore her choice was the tale of detection.

The form she chose, however, was more nearly the comedy of manners. The English novel of the nineteenth century had developed rich social types in concrete settings that provided shape for her own work. She loved to catch the accent, the tastes, the gestures of various folk in different situations, and to study their individual characteristics and their conformity to type. She loved British names—Thripp, Arbuthnet, Pettigrew-Robinson, Throgmorton, et al. Her careful research, therefore, was not limited to technical details of railway schedules or properties of poison, but also involved noting the people in the various regions, their occupations, eating habits, lodgings, and dress. And it demanded an ear for comic sounds and an eye for caricature.

Her decision to work in detective fiction was carefully calculated. She knew that the Anglo-Saxon people had a history of sympathy with the police, that they accepted the tradition of "fair play" for the criminal, that they enjoyed an intelligent central character, that they wanted good taste, a blend of romantic and classic form, and technical accuracy in even the smallest detail. She could feed these tastes while enjoying the pure analytic exercise detection involved and the rounded perfection of the tale of detection's form. Though it does not "and never can attain the loftiest level of literary achievement" and rarely touches the heights and depths of human passion, though it deals less with action than analysis and looks on death and mutilation with a dispassionate eye, it was nonetheless the form for her.[22]

The first of the Lord Peter Wimsey mysteries starts in proper epic fashion: *in medias res*, and in true thriller fashion: with a profane utterance. When Lord Peter says, "Oh, damn!" he is already a fully developed amateur sleuth, has already solved at least one important case, and is fully prepared by his reading (which mirrors his maker's) and his intellect (which excels hers in some ways) to solve any mystery put in his path. The discovery of a nude body (wearing only a pince-nez) found in an architect's bathtub is a proper challenge for the hero. The minimal evidence proves adequate to set the wheels going for this precise observer. Lord Peter, of course, is a delight. His artificiality is absurd, his tastes impeccable, and his powers outrageous: he has the eye of a falcon, an absolute understanding of every hint of psychology, a rapier wit, and of course delivers himself with studied understatement. Sayers keeps her audience at the point of barely suppressed laughter through much of the book with her mockery of the stale devices of detection and discovery.

This she blends with a subtle double vision, suggesting that the subject is not really funny, that the game is indeed deadly serious. Lord Peter admits to his friend Parker that he does enjoy the art of unraveling puzzles but not the necessary result of fixing on the criminals. He tends to enjoy the game only so long as he does not know either the villains or the victims. With sympathy and understanding come involvement and anguish; his disengaged mask drops off and his nerves explode.

For Parker, the Scotland Yard professional, the job is simpler: it is useful, suited to his talents, a work that encourages pride.[23] He insists that the sleuth cannot remain a West End dandy swaggering nonchalantly through a comedy constructed out of other people's pain. This is not a game like football, where one wins and then does the sporting thing. Though Lord Peter comes from a hunting family whose people never kill the fox, he cannot transfer this same sporting attitude to criminology. " 'You can't be a sportsman,' " Parker admonishes. " 'You're a responsible person.' "[24]

The novel reflects Peter's growing awareness of serious harm and of his own obligations. Though the book opens with the flippancy of an Oscar Wilde comedy, full of urbane wit, double entendres, and roguish unorthodoxy, we soon discover that Lord Peter is no decadent nihilist. Although his clothing may occasionally appear to be straight out of the mauve decade, his morality does not. His attention to superficial taste and appearance covers a deeper and finer taste and conscience. His frivolous manner masks a painful war experience and a feeling heart.

The comedy disappears entirely in the climactic scene, when Lord Peter looks in the eye of the murderer and sees there his willingness to repeat his crime. This man is no harmless fox to be hunted down for sport and released in the spirit of fair play. Crime is no game.

This is the recognition one might expect from an author who would later write feelingly of Satan and of hell. She does not take evil lightly.

She may not have many opportunities to make moral judgments in her advertising, but she certainly makes such opportunities in her novels.

The tone of comedy—in the classic sense of the goodness of the earth and the joy of people in it—is revived by the concluding scene. Lord Peter celebrates the cleansing of the world of this particular evil, the solution of this particular problem, by inviting the innocent (those deserving souls who did not murder Levy, though perhaps sorely tempted to do so) for dinner. Restoration of the society's health, not the recovery of its primal innocence, is the limited but valid basis for human celebration. "Not guilty" is the best verdict human justice can provide.

Sayers—given the circumstances of her life—could easily have become a misanthrope; but she never did. Increasingly she found herself amazed at the variety and enormity of human folly and stupidity, but she always saw much human decency and courage and gaiety as well. Since she was a young woman confronting the city, this attitude might be anticipated. That it continued even after her time of trial is a tribute to her ability to experience pain without turning sour.

Sayers is occasionally castigated for her anti-Semitism—ironically in the face of her long and happy relationship with a Jewish publisher, Gollancz. But in this novel, the slurs against the Jews are made not by the author but by unthinking characters. The dead man, a wealthy, middle-aged Jew, is presented as a simple, decent person—not a caricature. The murderer, not the author, is anti-Semitic here. Later on, she did use more reprehensible Semitic caricatures in her novels and short stories. And she wrote at least one article voicing alarm about the large Jewish immigration to England from Hitler's Germany. Some of her last efforts show a growing understanding of and respect for Jews, though she continued faintly to echo the worst form of British insularity in her snobbery. She always thought the Jews' faith to be erroneous in its denial of Christ's role as Messiah, but she finally came to respect Jesus' people for his sake. (See, for example, *The Man Born to Be King*, in which almost all the characters are Jews, and in which they and their faith are handled with respect.) Before coming to London, Sayers had probably never met any Jews; when she did, she found them a puzzle. Nancy-Lou Patterson has studied almost all of Sayers' published references to Jews, summing up her response as a "casual" snobbery, leading her to characterize Jews as being loyal to family rather than country, sharp in money transactions, and foreign in appearance. The very absence of Jews from much of British history, their late reappearance, and the quite recent enactment of the British acts of toleration had kept them a "small, compact community." The influx of Jews during World War I exacerbated British negative stereotypes, and the still larger immigration after the war seemed to some of the British to threaten Christianity and the Gentile community.

It is likely that Sayers would have joined those of the traditional stripe who are equally disturbed about the recent influx of so many people "of color" from different regions of the Empire. Though again not meant to be vicious, her references to "niggers" have the same unfortunate tone of stereotypes based on limited experience. Sadly, her well-stocked mind had the limitations and prejudices of her period. The vast world outside of England appeared to her as "alien," causing her to present Americans, Scots, and Europeans (apart from her beloved French) as comic or strange. Though she saw subtle variations in the English and the French, and would have screamed with laughter or outrage at a stereotype of the old maid or the career woman, she reduced others with unthinking snobbery to comic-strip characters.[25]

Whose Body? is an excellent introductory book for its portrayal of Lord Peter, his family, his friends, and his society. His essential helpers, Bunter and Parker, balance the dual nature of the hero. Bunter's exaggerated concern about creased trousers and proper decorum underscores Peter's dandyism, his frivolous nature. On the other hand, Parker, the theologian and intensely professional policeman, reminds us of Peter's more serious side. While Bunter keeps Peter *au courant* with newspapers and the latest books, Parker reminds him of enduring traditions, morality and faith. Parker prefers theology to poetry, morality to wit; he is thoughtful, insightful, careful, and scholarly—a restful counterbalance to Peter's whimsical cast of mind.

Each is in fact an extension of Sayers' own double personality. As she describes her process in creating character (in *The Mind of the Maker*), she says that she takes a facet of herself and expands, extends, and develops it. Sayers was always as middle-class as Parker, but her tastes were as elitist as Lord Peter's. She lived in small flats, often on back streets, but she loved the lavish country homes of the aristocracy.

She might sit alone at a cluttered kitchen table eating orange marmalade out of a tin while she made notes for her books, but she cherished the protocol and respected the cultivated palate of the epicure. Though she did not share in the wealth and perquisites of the aristocracy, she did not resent the British class system as so many of her contemporaries did. She was, in fact, a Tory to the end. The tradition she respected had a dignity and history she could appreciate even when her income was no longer derived from tithes nor her days spent in splendid cathedrals.

Her attitude toward the aristocracy reveals itself in her gentle handling of Lord Peter's family. His mother, the Dowager Duchess of Denver (Sayers delights in this alliteration), represents all that is sensible and good about British aristocracy. She has a keen wit, a sharp mind, an understanding of the power and the obligations of rank, and she has good taste in her display of wealth. She has read widely, but plays with her knowledge, confusing those who assume she is merely a silly old woman. Her bawdy Elizabethan humor, her generous love of Peter, and later of Harriet, and her open disapproval of the more fatuous members of her family make her a very winning character.

While we see in Lord Peter something of his mother's intellect and wit, her love of adventure, her common sense, and her awareness of the ridiculous, we see in Gerald and his stuffy wife all the worst aspects of British aristocracy. In time, we come to see this couple as unloving and unlovable, pompous, boorish, and bossy. Though the first novel reveals little of their human frailties, they are far more vividly portrayed in *Clouds of Witness* and *Busman's Honeymoon*. When we meet Gerald, the Duke of Denver, the peer who serves in the House of Lords, we realize why Sayers chose his younger brother for her hero. Gerald's rank and his constant awareness of his rank immobilize him, allowing him virtually no flexibility or fun—except that which he steals on the side. It is the aristocrat without the peerage, without the numerous residences to maintain, without the wife and family, who has the freedom to read his books, relish his wine, and seek his adventure.

Lord Peter's procedures for solving crimes are set up for us in *Whose Body?* Invariably, he selects a crime which has special interest for him. Detection is not an assignment but a challenge—often precipitated by a bit of whimsy (like the corpse being nude except for the glasses), or by a relationship to his own life or family, or by something that caught his attention. He always seeks to investigate the scene of the crime himself, though he is forced to rely on Bunter for the photographic record, Scotland Yard for the chemical analyses, and Charles Parker or Miss Climpson for most of the legwork. His role is the least technical, the most creative and the most fun. Sayers would see him as a type of scholar who makes the discoveries without the subsequent drudgery of footnoting or checking them.

The gathering process itself involves the narrowing of issues and setting of the problem to be solved. Generally the method is to discover first how it was done, then who did it, and finally why. After all, many people have motives for murder but never choose to act; so motive alone is not valuable evidence. Lord Peter tries to sort out the most likely suspects and learn as much as he can about them, not simply because of their motives, but because of their opportunity to commit the crime. But the central question is "how?" In the case of *Whose Body?* the "how" question involves how the corpse got into the bathtub. Then the following question is how the other body was disposed of—both the process and the timing. Only at the end does Peter discover why, a question both of specific motive and of the general psychology of the murderer.

The imaginative process involved in the problem-solving is almost poetic. Once his falcon's eye has noted the problems regarding the corpse, the scene, and the other elements surrounding the crime, he settles back to let them sink into his creative well. Discussions with witnesses, with friends and family, and reading help to settle and rearrange the ideas. His favorite method is to play the piano for long periods, then to leap up inspired and ready to pursue his proper course of action. Since we share the same information he has, we are invited to experience this pleasure of discovery with him.

Lord Peter is not a legalistic sort; he is convinced that people act out of their deepest religious, philosophic, and emotional commitments. Part of his research on suspected murderers is to read diaries, published books, and to listen closely to their words. A look in the eye or a fanatically held scientific theory can reveal an evil heart, the real cause of an evil act. He works from a Christian concept of human activity—the fruit revealing the true nature of the tree, even though he is not inclined to label his point of view Christian.

The second Wimsey novel, *Clouds of Witness*, develops the imagined world of Lord Peter far more fully, filling in details and demonstrating that the history and holdings of the family are formidable. The historian-scholar Sayers was thoroughly enjoying the witty elaboration of her mock-history of the British aristocrat. Eventually this game of pseudo-history was to involve her with a number of other people (particularly Mr. C. W. Scott-Giles, Fitzalan Pursuivant of Arms Extraordinary) who enjoyed helping Sayers as she created ("discovered") ancestors from different periods and histories. *Busman's Honeymoon* brings many of these family portraits together in a charming and comic mockery of British history. The game she was playing, and which others joined her in, demonstrates her irrepressible sense of fun and her delight in games, especially intellectual games using her rich scholarly resources.

Clouds of Witness, involving as it does a crime attributed to the Duke of Denver, Lord Peter's brother Gerald, necessarily presents the Wimsey family in more detail than the first novel. The Dowager Duchess is much more clearly a mother now, less a social character. She can spot her daughter's fake illness and straighten out her problems while she laughs at Freud and modern psychology. Again, in her garbled stream-of-consciousness monologues, we have insight into a delightfully shrewd mind, and a bawdy wit. Her speeches are an intellectual delight and an aesthetic triumph. Through her, Sayers can laugh at the cult of contemporaneity and laud the traditional values of maturity and antiquity. The Dowager Duchess is an aristocrat of the spirit, sympathetic, sensitive, sturdy, open to new values, but not quick to bow to the latest idol. Her generosity and common sense make us listen to her judgments carefully—as her son does—for she becomes a touchstone of rationality in the stories. We trust her evaluations of people and are inclined to agree with Peter in the later novels when he consults her in his growing admiration for Harriet Vane.

Peter's stuffy brother, the Duke of Denver, comes to life in this novel. The story deals with his arraignment and trial before the House of Lords on the charge of murder. Convinced that his aristocratic word is sufficient, the Duke is his own worst enemy. Blind to real values, he is willing to risk his life rather than risk his reputation; yet he was earlier willing to neglect that reputation in clandestine visits to a neighbor's wife. Not the sin itself but the public proclamation of it is his real worry. The best we can expect is that he will be able to cover his sins, not repent of them. This refusal to admit that on the night of the murder he stayed with another man's wife, who could easily establish his alibi, he calls "honor." He asserts that he is unwilling to sully her name, and Lord Peter hesitates to insist on public confession because of the probable effect on his family and the neighbor's. The woman's violently jealous husband threatens both Gerald and her. A British gentleman from beginning to end, Gerald can neither confess to his brother nor express his gratitude. The best his stunted soul can manage is a muttered word of thanks and a brief handshake. Sayers parodies British verbal and emotional understatement in Gerald—and makes us delight all the more in Peter's light touch, deep feelings, and verbal pyrotechnics.

The ebullient Peter, who cannot resist exchanging naughty limericks with a friend or tossing off a bawdy reference in the House of Lords, is a bundle of irreverence for revered traditions. Though their voices and appearances bear similarities, Peter and his brother are polar opposites. Peter can afford to be undignified, outspoken, frivolous, and flamboyant. It is characteristic that he would admit he loves Gerald and that he would sympathize with his affair, that he would be angry at his brother for risking his life, and that he would risk his own for him. As the "irresponsible" member of the family, he is not encased in the ermine robes (though Bunter is horrified that he appears without them and seeks to rectify the blunder as quickly as possible). His bachelor flat near Picadilly, his theatergoing, his manuscripts, and his flights across the Atlantic contrast with the vast estate at Denver, the unused library, the fox hunts, and the proper dinner parties of Gerald and his cardboard wife.

The family affair also involves Peter's young sister Mary, a girl with more physical appeal than her debonair brother, but less wit and common sense. While Peter accepts and enjoys the privileges of wealth and position, Mary resents and tries to reject them. A modern woman in her social ideas but not in her matrimonial ones, she is inclined to be a Shavian socialist. Though not so extreme in her dedication as Major Barbara, she does join the Soviet Club, and she serves as a nurse during the war. She has Gerald's sense of responsibility without his pleasure in position. A pretty woman—blond and slender—she is at the age when her destiny will lie in her choice of a mate. She is clearly not one who can find her proper work outside of helping a man do his work. In her selection of men, she shows consistently poor judgment, largely because of her muddled need for significant action. Her first choice is a vocal but cowardly activist, who would use her fortune while demanding her abasement before his self-proclaimed brilliance. The second is a burned-out, impoverished young *bon vivant* who would use her fortune to support his mistress. Mary is so determined to be of value to others that she fails to put any value on herself.

Again in Mary, her mother, even Peter and Gerald, we see facets of Sayers' life. Mary and Gerald in particular, with their confused and sad love affairs, seem to have been drawn from her own recent experiences. Dorothy Sayers, the maturing woman, was finding the aesthetic risks of Vanity Fair nowhere near so perilous as the moral and emotional ones. Her encounters with young men were apparently proving enlightening and painful.

We know from letters that she had discovered herself to be a "primitive woman" with primitive needs, not one who could live the life of the intellect alone.[26] And we know from correspondence now at Harvard University and from other sources that she found herself deeply in love with a minor novelist, John Cournos, who married soon after this time—shortly before she did. There were undoubtedly other objects of her unfocused passion as well. She was full of love, which she apparently offered with little discretion to an assortment of completely unworthy objects. Even more embarrassing, they rejected and humiliated her in various ways—or at least, so we must surmise from her novels and her subsequent activities. Without Lady Mary's wealth or physical beauty, she was doomed to experience an even more disappointed career in love. Sayers was understandably reticent to chronicle these painful years, forcing her public to follow her experience through its transformed shape in her fiction. She was living in a bohemian society, populated largely by single career women. The rare men who had survived the war were now comfortably married to women younger and prettier than she. A plain girl, eager for love and the experience of marriage, sensitive to rejection and abuse, obviously she risked being a victim in the sex game. T. S. Eliot describes the unfeeling sexuality of the period in *The Waste Land*, noting that love had been reduced to a game of chess. It is clear in *Clouds of Witness* and in succeeding Sayers books that she had come to a similar conclusion. She knew the disappointment of Eliot's Prufrock, who, when he has summoned the courage to ask the "overwhelming question" gets the bland and unfeeling response, "That is not what I meant, at all." She has known the same twilight streets that lead nowhere in the same "Unreal City." But she could not share the anaesthetized response of the typist who, in Eliot's "Fire Sermon," when deserted by her "carbuncular" clerk, sighs her empty and ironic response to "love," "Well, now that's done: and I'm glad it's over." Eliot makes much of the fact that the twentieth-century maiden who "stoops to folly and learns too late that men betray" simply turns to put another record on the gramophone. The new liberated women, confronted by no sense of sin and no depth of emotion, find only weariness and death in loveless lust. They need a healing hand, a cleansing fire, "death by water," to renew them, to touch them with new love, and to lead them back to renewal and hope. Sayers says much less than Eliot by way of explicit commentary on the age; she simply portrays it. In the midst of her own experience of profane love, she was not ready with an easy spiritual or intellectual solution. But neither does she seem to have grown bitter.

It is pleasing to notice that Charles Parker is quietly in love with Mary for her real virtues—not just her lovely face, but her serious, generous, and courageous nature. He has the intellectual discipline and sense of vocation that can bring direction to her life. And he is so scrupulous that he would never touch her fortune or abuse her faith. Their courtship is to take years, but Sayers seems to think that for such a woman as this, marriage is the best path. The Christian Parker will seek from this spark of love to build a solid relationship before he will dare to speak of marriage—and only then because Peter pushes him to do so.

The whole book centers on love and lust. While Parker's growing love for Mary forms a steady rhythm all through the story, Peter's diminishing love for Barbara (the girl who earlier rejected him) balances in a chiasmatic (x-shaped) structure. In the foreground is the frenzied whirl of passion and the formal dance of mating. The dreary marriage of Gerald and his imperial Duchess is paralleled by the arid courtship of Mary and her dissipated Denis. Behind this masque of ritual responsibility is the passionate subterfuge of each. Gerald sneaks off in the night to visit his beautiful neighbor. Mary plots a nocturnal elopement with her radical lover. Neither passion turns out to amount to much when considered in the clear light of day. And both intrigues involve the siblings in violence and deceit. The modest message seems to be that illicit passion has few joys and great sorrows. The product does not live up to the advance advertisements.

Lord Peter, in his search for the truth about his family, discovers a great deal about their lives, their minds, and their emotions. And because they are so closely kin to him, he consequently finds out a lot about himself—a path of self-discovery that will culminate in *Gaudy Night.* The Wimsey tribe does not find happiness easily and cannot be content without love; they need more than the empty ceremony, they need the experience itself. Gerald is too tradition-bound to continue his search, but Mary and Peter do continue to experiment, grow, and learn.

Unfortunately for her personal contentment (and perhaps fortunately for her art), Dorothy Sayers found no Charles Parker (or Lord Peter) waiting nearby to love and protect her. She could not pretend to be a helpless Lady Mary, a broken lily who could appeal to a hero's manliness and sympathetic nature. If the suspicions of the biographers and the details of the records in Somerset House are correct, Dorothy Sayers found herself pregnant and unmarried at about this time. This was certainly the ultimate horror for the rector's daughter, one that would have precipitated lamentations and perhaps suicide attempts with other people. We can only speculate that Sayers established the facts, analyzed her options, and plotted her path with a remarkably cool head. She probably told her parents, bought baggy clothing (or perhaps used the more disreputable parts of her own never-elegant wardrobe), sought six months' leave from her employer, ostensibly to finish a novel, got on her motorcycle, and rode home to have her baby, which she bore in a nursing home in Bournemouth on January 3, 1924. James Brabazon insists that the father was not anyone of public significance nor was he either Cournos or the man Sayers later married. We do not know whether hopes for marriage or passionate lamentations were a part of this domestic tragedy. It is hard to believe that the experience was so matter-of-fact as it appears in retrospect from the meager records. Undoubtedly, when she laughs in a letter about the ease with which one may go through pregnancy undetected (she said that all it takes is "plenty of guts and a powerful constitution"), she is being "gallant and gay" in the face of very real distress.[27] The experience was certainly the greatest personal challenge Sayers ever confronted. It would appear from the records that she faced it with dignity and courage and self-control and a sense of personal responisbility.

She apparently registered the birth, christened the boy John Anthony, and arranged for his keep with an eccentric cousin, Ivy Shrimpton, who had been a childhood friend, a spinster who sounds a bit like Miss Climpson.[28] Then she returned briskly to work and to life, perhaps even to love. The book that she wrote in part during the six months' leave of absence from Benson's was *Clouds of Witness.*

The book is certainly an interesting one to have been written when she was discovering herself to be without husband and with child. The story is hardly an epithalamion, a celebration of the joys of love or marriage. The toughness of its views on illicit affairs, on courtship, love, and marriage, suggests that a subtle and complex philosophy of ideal male-female relationships was evolving in her mind. The sexual drive is a clear motivating force for most of the characters, but Dorothy L. Sayers has little respect for sex alienated from love. Lord Peter, preferring to wait for love (in spite of his liberal French sex education), looks a lot more attractive in his responsible self-control than the lascivious Denis and his cynical mistress. In this story, Sayers pictures men and women exploiting one another in particularly ugly ways. She pictures romatic love in a jaundiced manner. The wellspring of passion within the human is powerful indeed. When it is triggered by physical beauty and fed by deceit, it is hardly a solid basis for a lasting relationship, a real marriage.

The marriages in the story—Gerald and his lady or the neighbor Grimethorpe and his—are not satisfactory alternatives to the illicit affairs. One is boring and the other is brutal. Neither family finds joy in its day-to-day life. By contrast, Mary, in her puzzled search for meaning and love in marriage, is on the right track. She is not wildly in love with Parker yet, nor even especially romantic in her expressions even after they marry, but she does have hopes that sex, romance, and marriage can combine with modest success. With patience and affection, men and women can over the long run form a rich community of mutual love and support.

Dorothy Sayers' many meditations on love, sacred and profane, would have been less likely products of a contented woman, happily married and surrounded by her children and her chores. Adversity challenged her thoughts as well as her actions, toughening her and forcing her deeper and deeper into the contemplation of the psychology and theology of love. Without such an experience in sin and its consequences, Dorothy L. Sayers would probably have been as limited in her perceptions of emotional truth as she was in her sensitivity to racial and national differences. She grew more subtle and more modest in her analyses of evil as she confessed by hint and indirection that she did indeed know something of the experience of sin. This period was a turning point for her, demanding a humble reconsideration of her ethics and her theology. Frequently hereafter she was to note the good that comes out of evil—without pretending to excuse the evil itself. She was to have at least one more significant opportunity to see God bringing all things together for good for those who love him. Having deliberately chosen the challenging life of the warfaring world, she had to expect defeats and wounds along the way. A cloistered life would have stifled her; the challenge of battle spurred her on to new heights.

Sayers' biography remains clouded regarding these years. Whether out of an understandable fear of her society which had no sympathy for fallen women, or a responsibility to protect her parents, or a belief that her life was her own business, or the simple delight of creating and maintaining a mystery, she never chose to clear the picture. She certainly left the impression that she bore an illegitimate son in 1924, whom she later adopted, educated, and named her heir—Anthony Fleming. She took a leave of absence from her job at Benson's, returned to her family at Christchurch, and perhaps produced a child. Janet Hitchman and Ralph Hone both found public records of a child born to "Dorothy Sayers, authoress, of 24 Great James Street, London."[29] But, as another scholar, Dr. Bonnie Heintz, noted in a private conversation, such evidence is suspect. Sayers invariably insisted on her middle initial, partly because she was proud of her mother's family and partly because she did not want to be confused with a "second-rate actress'' named Dorothy Sayers. She would never have used the feminine form of the noun for her profession, and usually identified herself as ''writer.'' She refused to discuss the parentage of this son during her lifetime, even with him or her closest friends. The child might have been hers or he might have been a friend's. Sayers never told him, according to Bonnie Heintz, who is now at work on a life of Sayers. But the official biographer, James Brabazon, insists that there are letters proving the birth of the child to Sayers and identifying the father—who was not the man Sayers eventually married. Both Hitchman and Brabazon, and the most recent biographers, Alzina Dale and Ralph Hone, agree the child was raised by a spinster cousin, Ivy Shrimpton, and never lived with Dorothy L. Sayers.

Regardless of the facts—which are only the limited and temporary details of human life—the literature, a more universal and permanent record, shows Dorothy L. Sayers knowledgeable about love, lust, courtship, and marriage. A good reader can certainly pick up a sex education from books, but we have no guarantee that this thirty-year-old unmarried woman living among bohemian circles in London relied entirely on books. Sayers clearly enjoyed the company of men, was a thoroughly womanly woman, and was not the least shocked by lust. She thought it ranked lower among the sins than gluttony or sloth or pride—sins that were more dangerous to other people and more damaging to one's own soul. She cherished her personal privacy and stoutly maintained that the life of the artist had no bearing on the value of the book. What she wanted us to know about herself, she told us in her voluminous writings.

Unlike St. Augustine or St. Theresa, she was not prepared to bare her soul and her life in a spiritual autobiography. With proper British reticence, she continued to assert (against much contrary evidence) that her stories were not autobiographical. The biographical dictionaries of the period refer to her adopted son and her idyllic life. Janet Hitchman raised a great storm of dismay with her disclosure of the hidden anguish and sorrow of this woman. Sayers' own decision was to take the neoclassical path: to ignore the individual, idiosyncratic facts, to develop a universal statement, and to keep the artist separate from the work. Whether the choice was self-serving (an act of moral cowardice) or heroic (an act of aesthetic purism), it was firm and unswerving. She paid a significant price for her silence, but she was strong enough to face solitary suffering and dignified enough to resent public display of dirty linen. In later years, when she might have had occasion to use her experience to help others, she was too famous to risk scandal. The private person could have damaged the public works. And it would have embarrassed her as much as it would Lord Peter to indulge in public confession or breast-beating. So her secret was buried with her, but her books record her changing moods.

The bitterness of the works that followed immediately after *Clouds of Witness* suggests that she knew a period of deep distress. But for Lord Peter and for Dorothy Sayers, love was much too important to ignore. Peter found that his healing took years, but the healthy human is amazingly resilient. Time does mercifully cover over scars and allows new hope to flourish.

III. Through the Valleys

Like Bunyan's pilgrim, Dorothy L. Sayers went through the Valley of Humiliation and confronted Apollyon. And like him, she was forced to reply to the "foul fiend" who insisted that she had now entered his country and was his subject. She was forced to admit, like Christian, that she was almost "choked in the Gulf of Despond," that she did "attempt wrong ways" to be rid of her burden, and that she did "sinfully sleep, and lose" her choice thing. She too has been "inwardly desirous of vainglory" in all that she said and did. But she, like Christian, knew the way back to the King's Highway, because "the Prince whom I serve and honour is merciful and ready to forgive."[1]

The experience of humiliation deepened Sayers' thinking, helped her start on the path toward a more mature system of thought, forced her to admit that the intellect alone is insufficient. It forced her into a reconsideration of a number of subjects: love, law, morality, tradition, women's roles, and of course marriage.

She had originally presented her hero as a rebel within limits; she now used him as an increasingly thoughtful rebel. Through him, she considered the importance of tradition and the necessity of individualism in a society. She had always been in love with tradition and at odds with it, in her religion, her education, and her view of self. Now, feeling an outcast (psychologically if not socially), she turned to a consideration of British tradition and law. Amazingly, though, she did not weep and demand our sympathy; she laughed at the shallowness of cherished ideals. Her continuing love for British tradition and amusement at it appear in her mock-heroic handling of the trial before the House of Lords (in *Clouds of Witness*). The presentation is a model of formality, pomp, and foolishness. But behind all the protocol lurks a partially discovered truth. Though Gerald's values are foolish and his behavior reprehensible, his decorum is appealing. In an age like ours, when authors' confessions of their private lives are so frequently sold as plays or novels for audiences delighted at the chance for legalized gossip and voyeurism—in such a time of sensationalism and self-advertisement, the Duke of Denver's reticence is dignified and refreshing. It speaks of Dorothy L. Sayers' own respect for privacy. Though she used her experiences to shape her art, she refused to advertise herself by public confessions.

The question of public confession is thoroughly probed in *Clouds of Witness*. If Gerald were to confess his affair, he would clear himself of more serious charges, but he would (in all likelihood) damage his mistress's reputation, marriage, and health. The argument might well be made that he shows more concern for these precious commodities after the fact than before. His motives are indeed clouded; we know he respects his own reputation far more than hers. But any confession of illicit love which names the other person forces the partner into the limelight unwillingly. The adultery had already damaged her marriage; the publicity would damage it still further. Yet adultery is likely to occur only when marriage is already on the rocks. No romantic vision of noble motives or undying love clouds this analysis. The wicked couple do not race off to sea in hopes of a freer life on a South Sea Island. They cynically take up their old lives or find new solutions apart from the "beloved." They are unloving and selfish to the end. Their options do not include a return to primal innocence, and they do not consider a baptism of fire and water.

Sayers' irrepressible laughter, even in this bitter book, turns back upon herself, with some hint of her own pain. Lady Mary exaggerates the importance of each affair in her life; Lord Peter thinks that his being jilted by a little fluff is the central tragedy of his life. But they gradually regain the perspective to realize that they are part of a pattern within the massive sweep of human history: their pain is both typical and temporary. Over the years, Sayers was to continue to investigate this tension between tradition and the individual, the collective and the private, culminating in her fascinating studies of Dante. That she intended this second Lord Peter novel to signify more than the false charges brought against Gerald is signaled by the Biblical title: *Clouds of Witness*. The title alludes to the declaration in Hebrews that we are not alone in our suffering, our "mocking and scourging." For "we are surrounded by so great a cloud of witnesses" that we may "lay aside every weight, and sin which clings so closely." Therefore, "let us run with perseverance the race that is set before us, looking to Jesus the pioneer and perfecter of our faith, who for the joy that was set before him endured the cross, despising the shame, and is seated at the right hand of the throne of God." (Heb. 11:36; 12:1–2) Although Sayers does not turn the book into a private statement or a theological one, she provides evidence of the undergirding of her faith and the concerns of her life in both her approach and her title.

Her continuing interest in a "just vengeance" is also a theme of *Clouds*. From her earliest poems to her last works on Dante, including a play by the title *The Just Vengeance*, she worried over the ideas of anger, retribution, crime, law, and morality. Lawyers and law courts are given considerable space in this novel, culminating in the properly celebrated scene in the House of Lords. Placed in this structure of human justice, which rolls along with its attorneys, judges, inspectors, coroners, and ordinary police through its procedures of investigation, arraignment, incarceration, defense, trial, judgment, and execution, is the solitary human culprit. The accused cannot help feeling a victim, for no one is really innocent. And the system does seem ponderous and inhuman. Sayers tries to show a variety of human types within the system that modify it: The family lawyer, Mr. Murbles, is gently human, even willing on occasion to unbend his mouth into a smile acknowledging a witticism. Sir Impey Biggs, the trial attorney, is more flamboyant, more handsome, more eloquent, more fun, and less scrupulous about truth. Lord Peter listens to a conversation between the lawyers regarding how the jury can be confused and the accused man freed, to which he responds: " 'I've always said . . . that the professional advocate was the most immoral fellow on the face of the earth, and now I know for certain.' "[2]

The final judgment in the book avoids the issue of moral guilt, for this is not to be determined in a court of law. The full truth is not even sought; it is irrelevant to the case at hand. Gerald is innocent of this crime, but not innocent in the fuller way. With this awareness, Lord Peter cannot end this experience in evil with a celebration of human goodness. He and his friends conclude *Clouds of Witness* with a night of drunken revelry—human affection and forgetfulness are his antidotes for the painful awareness of human sin.

The book does not, in fact, deal with crime, but violence against self. Denis Cathcart is not the only one who turns on himself and does the greatest possible damage to his own life. The unhappy loves of this book all twist themselves into some kind of violence against self. In the most humiliating experiences of life, we need no court of law to condemn us. We punish ourselves. Later, in her discussion of Dante's Hell, she made this point with great clarity. We are not placed in hell, we place ourselves there by our desires and actions. We define ourselves in our life and choose to go to our own proper sphere thereafter. God's goodness is the measure by which we are judged guilty, the plumb line that displays our crookedness.

Dorothy Sayers also shows how the greatest harm comes from the inside, not the outside adversary. The Giant Despair has his castle conveniently located in our hearts. The real battle is within, and the real violence most of us know is violence against ourselves. Sin itself is a kind of self-destruction, by which we mangle the image of God in us and cast ourselves out of Eden. Her discussions suggest she blamed herself for her problems. There is no evidence she ever asked or received any help from the child's father. And she never attacked him publicly except through the portraits of unloving, weakly handsome users of women. Clearly she placed the blame fully on the ample shoulders of that responsible young woman Dorothy Leigh Sayers.

Though *Clouds of Witness* talks about justice, it does not preach or make explicit reference to it. It opens with Peter's explorations of the vendetta in its "native habitat"—Corsica, and concludes with his provisional acceptance of the more domesticated British form of vengeance, justice. But the foreshadowing is obvious. Lord Peter will have increasing difficulty with human law and human justice.

In the next book, *Unnatural Death*, Lord Peter begins to worry in earnest about legality in general and his own ethics in particular. His flippant decision to inquire unasked into an apparently innocent death ends in the uncovering of a crime and the triggering of several others. Although Lord Peter sees little harm in killing a terminally ill patient who is suffering terribly with cancer, Mr. Tredgold, the priest in the story, argues that we have no right to take life and death so arrogantly into our own hands. The damage is not so much to society as to the killer. Such actions lead one to believe one is above all laws, and then society itself cannot be safe. He comforts Lord Peter by assuring him that he is not serving a "private vengeance" but social good; thus he is justified in his actions so long as he does his best in accordance with the laws. The good priest admonishes him to recognize that we all fall short of the justice of God. In short, he tells Peter to do justly, love mercy, and walk humbly with his God.[3]

Lord Peter is depressed much of the way through *Unnatural Death*, and even more so at the conclusion when he hears that the convicted criminal has hanged herself. But Parker, who always has his eye on the sun, realizes that the darkness of the day is temporary—an eclipse—and that the brightness will return.

Sayers also continues her commentary on lawyers, expanding on the character of Murbles and developing others. She enjoys having them sound like their own briefs, playing with legal terms, cross-examining one another, delighting in their subtle interpretations. Like the detective with all his self-defeating complexity, the law here precipitates the violence by its failure to be simple and reasonable. A change in terminology results in a foolish change in the line of inheritance, causing the property to go to the state when it was clearly intended for the niece. This inhumane legalism cannot be relieved at the end of the novel, and is of course the reason that the solar eclipse on the last page depresses Lord Peter unreasonably. It would appear that society is blind and God is hiding his face from us.

Unnatural Death, the third Wimsey novel, predictably expands still more on the family and personality of Lord Peter. The "Biographical Note," added after 1954, gives much fuller explanations of the war background, the youth and education of the man, and the influence of his wayward uncle Paul. The disclosure of his sexual and romantic background prepares the way for his further considerations of love and marriage in the later novels. Wimsey's education and development of vocation—the precocious child, the aesthetic adolescent, the cultivated adult—remind us a great deal of his maker and of her characterization of the stages of growth in her advocacy of the trivium. Instead of a witty and brittle member of the decadent generation, we find him to be increasingly a complex and sensitive person, a scholar and a gentleman.

It is interesting that his education in sex was in France, as her own may well have been. Experimentation in the "arts of love" is considered an asset for the urbane gentleman and a shame for the fallen woman. The double standard is obvious, but Sayers does not dwell on it. She later remarks that women are judged exclusively for their sexual or sex-related qualities, while men are allowed to be more fully human. She does not seek to be—like the medieval lady—far above man to inspire him, nor—like the *femme fatale*—far beneath him to corrupt him.[4] She really wants to be the main event, not adjunct to man at all. Certainly such a woman as this, growing plump and prematurely middle-aged with her thin hair and thick glasses, must have chafed at the constant and unrelenting judgment of her "womanliness." There was so much more to Dorothy L. Sayers than her sexuality, and that was so often tainted by being trapped in such an unaesthetic body. Though she opposed the woman's being constantly regarded as a sex-object, she must have found her own failure to be seen as sexually appealing a great distress. Not being a sex-object in a world that values women for their sexuality is even more painful than being one. Lord Peter could offer a welcome escape from the whole ridiculous trap; in him she could enjoy the full development of a whole human being, with the sexual nature serving only as a single part of a complex whole.

An even more explicit statement on women appears in Lord Peter's new associate, Miss Climpson. She is introduced in a delightfully comic scene. Lord Peter has impishly encouraged Parker to anticipate that he is about to meet Peter's mistress, though Peter has not used just those words. Instead of the expected beauty, the inspector finds Miss

Climpson, a "thin, middle-aged woman, with a sharp, sallow face and very vivacious manner."[5] A spinster raised by her Victorian family to be an asset to the drawing room rather than the office, she was discouraged in her early ambition to be a lawyer. She now finds herself in middle age sans husband, sans resources, sans drawing room, and amazingly sans bitterness. In the chapter's heading, Dorothy L. Sayers notes ironically that there are two million more females than males in England—" 'an awe-inspiring circumstance.' "[6] She obviously expects her audience to see Miss Climpson as a representative of the generation that, by the way, includes the spinster Sayers among its members.

Since Victorian and Edwardian English men as a rule encouraged women to consider marriage as their only proper expectation in life, all of these spinsters were excluded *a priori* from the life that society had defined as the only one with meaning. Sayers saw this attitude as being responsible for an enormous waste of human resources. She was sympathetic with spinsters and middle-aged women of nondescript appearance for obvious reasons, including a maiden aunt who lived with her for years and a spinster cousin who watched over her son. Vera Brittain recalls that Florence Nightingale was also outraged by the "suffocating elegance of a Victorian drawing room. 'Why have women passion, intellect, moral activity—these three—and a place in society where no one of the three can be exercised?' "[7]

Sayers had known brilliant women whose lives were horribly stunted by the narrow bounds they thought proper to explore. They were often the unconscious prisoners of a middle-class morality; women in the lower classes were rarely forbidden to work outside the home. Even those few upper- and middle-class women who actually found their way to colleges and studied for the law or other careers were often excluded from the examinations or from the profession itself by a hostile, male-dominated world. Just as Sayers herself had been denied a degree for almost a decade, others had been denied far more than a degree for a far longer time. Women could still not hope to enter into or succeed in many professions, and English women at this time were still denied the vote. Those who dared to reject the path of matrimony because of their ambitions or because of their failure to find appropriate mates were often treated as social pariahs. The old actress in *Strong*

Poison and the spinster horse-breeders in *Unnatural Death* pay the price of social ostracism for their independent career choices. Dorothy L. Sayers must have drawn some of her inspiration for such portraits from her sympathetic observation of the talented and unmarried members of her beloved "Mutual Admiration Society."

The Victorian era had seen great changes in opportunities for and attitudes toward women, but many more were needed before they could achieve anything approaching their full potential. Undoubtedly, Sayers' new experience among men at work and in society convinced her that they were by no means superior creatures who warranted the adoration of self-abasing women. She knew her talents to be superior to those of her male co-workers as often as not. In a gentle manner she tentatively develops in *Unnatural Death* some of her ideas on the "right kind of feminism." This book and others quietly present the tragedies of wasted women; these ideas are even more explicit in *Gaudy Night* and *Are Women Human?* Yet she never became an antagonist to men. Though she did find herself pressed to point out the ironies in society's stunting of women and then its finding fault with their being stunted, and though she did satirize with some astringency the chauvinists (though she would never have used the term) and the perpetrators of doublethink, especially those who profess to be Christian, she never turned against the middle class, the British Victorian culture, or the church. Like her Miss Climpson, she remains an unabashed and fervent Anglo-Catholic, who is conservative, emotional, and traditional in her religion. Miss Climpson's gossipy letters to Lord Peter, annotated with underlinings and parentheses as if they were musical scores, are invariably in part thoughtful meditations on sin and salvation. They are not attacks on society or tracts for the times. The failure of individual Christians to acknowledge the full humanity of women does not—for Miss Climpson or Dorothy Sayers—deny the value of the church itself. After all, Christ himself saw women as fully human—but he was a man unlike other men.[8]

One of the more daring ideas in *Unnatural Death* is the perversion of feminism—turning from the love of men to the love of other women. In what Miss Climpson calls her "woman-ridden" existence, an existence Sayers shared for the first twenty-five years of her life, she had seen many levels of woman-love. The deep friendship of school chums, which often ripens into a mature partnership, may provide a community of affection and mutual support for women. Sayers herself found this among the "Mutual Admiration Society," that group of Oxford women she continued to love for the rest of her life. A school-girl crush on an older woman or teacher is a more adolescent and fragile outcropping of the romantic drive, and one which has more dangers. She shows one such case in which the older woman manipulates the younger, exploiting her naivete and loyalty, and demanding that she despise men and reject marriage.

Miss Climpson makes no overt judgments on lesbian love (though Lord Peter does), but she does delicately recommend that male-female love is better and more "fruitful." She at the same time notes that possessive love of another human can easily slide over into idolatry—even Milton's "he for God only, and she for God in him."[9] This consideration of the proper role of human love was to grow increasingly complex in the later studies. In a very frank discussion, Miss Climpson admits that men often find friendships among themselves to be less claustrophobic, easier and more comfortable because they generally have more outside interests than women and are therefore likely to be less demanding on the emotional level.

Among the intelligentsia of Bloomsbury at this time, Sayers could not help but notice the complex and perverse variations of love. The communities of lovers, arrangements in threes, and homosexual variations were becoming notorious. In the more sophisticated novels of the time by Aldous Huxley or Virginia Woolf, we see the experiments presented in witty, sensitive, and aesthetically alluring terms. On a different level, the period also saw the novels of D. H. Lawrence, the patron saint of primal, sensual love, whom Sayers later satirized caustically on her "Pantheon Papers" plate with the inscription: "Fiery Loins of St. Lawrence, D. H." His powerful novels of love and lust had enormous impact on contemporary thought, and his notion of love's "rainbow" must have appealed to Sayers. (She quotes him in *The Documents in the Case.*) But his arch (for he too was a student of cathedrals) was Norman: it turned back toward the earth. Hers was Gothic: it pointed toward heaven.

The lesbian love in *Unnatural Death* runs its distorted path through egoism and violence toward death. Miss Climpson, a spinister "made and not born—a perfectly womanly woman''[10] laments the anguish of the woman-ridden life, full of passionate scenes and slighted affection, jealousy and anger and frustration,[11] and pronounces it unhealthy. She argues with narrow-minded men who would limit women's use of their own lives, and she makes the best possible use of her own. But her expectations and demands for adventure and passion are modest; she is a self-deprecating lady of great wisdom and dignity and faith.

Sayers' own life for the moment was haunted with choices between love of women, love of men, lust, and marriage, and it was inevitable that her concerns should enter her writing. But she was destined to consider passion in any case; it is the most common motive for violence. Most often in her stories, the love is perverse or excessive (using Dante's categories) rather than natural and balanced. Possessive love particularly disturbs her for its distortion of lives along with its bland self-serving self-justification as being ''Christian'' or ''romantic.'' She wrote her meditations on cruel and possessive love at the same time she was preparing to marry. Her numerous friends, many of them male, may have contributed to her comments on the selfish and abusive love life among the bohemian community. But even in the village, her lovers tend to damage one another.

We have only spotty records of her break with the earlier love and the courtship of the new, but references suggest a prolonged period of contentiousness. For years she had spent her life holding out her love to one man after another like a bouquet that each in turn refused. She continued against all contrary evidence in her own experience to believe in the redemptive power of natural love. And she very probably thought she has at least found equal affection, though unequal intellect, in the dashing military man who had entered her life.

He was some years older than she, divorced, less successful in his writing, but handsome and charming—and she was in no position to be choosy. It may well be a tribute to her hope for a new life that she speaks of rejecting unnatural loves at this point in favor of wholesome married love. She was in her thirties, increasingly successful, increasingly certain of her own intellectual abilities. Pictures disclose her to have been overweight and bespectacled. It does not take much to encourage the human appetite for love. There is no reason, she thought, that love should be restricted to the very young and the very slim and the very beautiful. She was quite ready to believe that her dark period was only an eclipse of her sun.

Out of proper and natural love comes new life—literally and figuratively. *Unnatural Death* notes that out of distorted loves, by contrast, comes violence to self and to others. Out of the unnatural life comes the unnatural death. The fact of a criminal action may be enough for the courts, but the church and Christians are more concerned with intention. If the heart is full of anger, the hand acts in the violence. And the fruit of the action proves the nature of the tree. When no actual crime has been committed, motive does not matter in law. But in life, the souring and distorting that precede action are also important.

Lord Peter's increasing seriousness about his work and the issues it raises makes him less witty, less dandified, less a disinterested, objective observer of the comedy of life. In this novel, both he and Miss Climpson see evil in the eyes of the criminal. He feels the lesbian cringe at his touch, and uses intuition more than intellect in his pursuit of the truth. At the end, he discovers his own complex mind has been his worst enemy in solving the problem: he overlooked what was ridiculously simple while he concocted exotic solutions. Sayers' point is a good one: the intellectual may miss the obvious truth, confused by the intellect itself. (This perversion of the intellect was to become the seed for her later study of Judas.)

Overreliance on the intellect turned out to be Dorothy Sayers' own worst failing. She found to the very end of her life that she was too cerebral to be an evangelical Christian. Later in her life, she was to write a friend, "I do not know whether the intellect can save itself. I can be saved by nothing else."[12] Hers was the passionate intellect that dominated life, making ideas more real to her than the events themselves or the people who precipitated them. Her faith in the intellect sometimes led her into logical conclusions without adequate emotional bases, and she was honest enough to recognize this flaw in herself.

Her private life at this time, though, was so torn by emotion that she was forced into a recognition of the impressive power of irrational forces. She places the use of psychology and intuition neatly into her stories. But even when she is proclaiming the role of the irrational, she cannot truly abandon her mind or her art to it. The weakest scenes in her books are those that threaten to become most emotional—the nervous breakdowns, visions, dreams, etc. She avoids the problem with love scenes by having her characters talk their way through them; seldom does she describe gestures or linger on the passion itself. Her best success is with comedy, understatement, and dialogue. She can use a symbolic gesture and then indulge herself in a philosophical analysis of the feelings, thus avoiding close encounters of the nonverbal kind. Her easiest and most natural successes are those cerebral moments where witty dialogue and ironic situation delight and challenge the intellect.

Her appetite for intellectual food probably made her unattractive to those with less voracious appetites and less discriminating tastes. She is said not to have suffered fools gladly. Inclined to be short with the dull and the pompous, to argue with more vigor than the occasion merited, she could hardly have made a satisfactory or ego-building wife for a man less intelligent or honest than she. Unfortunately, she seldom met an eligible man as intelligent or as talented or as forthright. Her increasingly peppery manner was the by-product of her great mind and her pride in the intellect. Even as a girl, writing home to her family, she had noted perceptively, "I must have a man who will fight me."[13] Her declaration of need became an ironic prophecy: she insisted on having a man, and the man she found did indeed fight her, but never with the proper weapons. She recognized the flaw of her own intellectual pride, she discussed it numerous times, but she never overcame it.

The dark days and the exploration of the Valley of the Shadow continued into the next novels, especially *The Unpleasantness at the Bellona Club*, Sayers' war novel. It is set in a club named for the goddess of war; and the murder takes place on an Armistice Day some years after the Great War, when Lord Peter, a war veteran, is well into his thirties. He has been deeply scarred, as have others in the club: notably George, a man whose nerves were permanently shattered, and his brother Robert, a career military man, who has been inhumanly hardened by war. Robert is able to endure the horrors of the trenches, face death, and ignore morality. Sayers suggests that a sensitive conscience is almost impossible in the violent scramble for survival. It is no wonder that she has one of her characters comment on the universal impact of World War I. Not only did it kill off, mutilate, and harden a whole generation of men, but it robbed, warped, and hurt a corresponding generation of women—Sayers' generation.

The Oxford years had been barren of men (reducing the male population of the university from 3,000 to 350, taking even the male faculty away), the Bloomsbury years not much better. A vast number of men had been killed in the Great War, an incredible loss for England. For men, a war novel usually involves the battlefield or the escape from it (like *The Red Badge of Courage* or *A Farewell to Arms* or *Catch-22*). For women it would be quite different unless the heroine chose to be a nurse or a partisan warrior—as in Hemingway's novels. The millions of women like Miss Climpson and Miss Sayers were war casualties of a more lingering, less heroic sort.

The most important impact of the war on the mature Sayers was her marriage to a war veteran—or a man reported to have been a war correspondent. In 1926, when she was thirty-three years old, Dorothy L. Sayers married Oswald Atherton Fleming (usually referred to as "Mac") in a civil ceremony at the Registry. He was a divorced man with children, thought to have been a captain (probably because of his own claims), and a war victim of sorts. The records are confused and neglected on Fleming. Janet Hitchman doubts that he was a war hero and suggests that he was more of a lazy and shiftless drunk than a romantic victim of gassing, but no one can quite tell from the records. His writings were not signed (though Ralph Hone has located some of them),[14] and his war record was not singled out for special notice. As a soldier he must have had limited and unspectacular experience, the only thing remaining to tell us about his war life being a copy of his *How to See the Battlefields*. Of the afteryears, only a cookbook remains. Miss Hitchman, after searching the records, decided he was a fraud, a lecher, and a parasite. Friends and family insist on the contrary that he was a bright, genial man terribly altered by the war.

Fleming's daughter Ann, in a letter on file in the Sayers archives at Roslyn House, disagrees strongly with Hitchman's characterization of her father as an "utter rogue" looking for a "cushy billet." She notes that Sayers was not wealthy, that both she and Fleming's first wife were intelligent women, and that neither woman was the sort to have "loved and married a 'shallow' man." She also believes that he did some writing no longer available because unsigned. He did work some in his early years for industry, and he was something of a photographer, and he may have done work not credited to him.

Ann's were slight and pleasant memories of a man who made a modest living from his work as a free-lance writer, who loved history and machinery and photography. He had two daughters by his first marriage, which Ann remembers as idyllic for some years. He built an airplane and a summer house, and apparently enjoyed working with his hands. He and his brothers volunteered for the army at the beginning of the war, and both of his brothers were killed in it. Ann Fleming Schreurs notes that her father wrote some articles about the war and the battlefields, but was not actually a war correspondent.

Her father did not return to the family after the war. He worked in London, for an advertising agency that she suspects was Benson's and lived at Grey's Inn. He never, as she recalls, was the same person again, never returned to become a part of his family. By 1924, he had stopped supporting them. Even when his wife divorced him, he seldom met the alimony payments and no longer showed any interest in the family. His daughter suspects that the break with the family was partly the result of war traumas and partly the meeting with Dorothy Sayers. He did not tell the family about his marriage or seek to keep in contact with his children. His daughter believes that his new wife blocked any relationship with the old family, and characterizes Sayers as possessive and "powerful." Fleming did not even respond to a letter in 1932 from his dying daughter Mary, telling him that she was ill and did not expect to recover. Ann suspects that he never received the letter and hints darkly that his new wife kept it from him. Ann made some attempts to see her father shortly before his death, but found him to be "upset" at any reference to the past.

Whatever the real motives and psychology and activity behind this bizarre and apparently cruel and irresponsible behavior, it is clear that Fleming was damaged psychologically by the war and the loss of his brothers. The complete transformation of character and the estrangement from family (even before his association with Sayers) could hardly be attributed to the malign influence of a woman he met and married some years later. Rather, it would appear he was the husk of a man by the time Dorothy Sayers met him—already middle-aged, careless about his family, floating from job to job, confused by the horrors of war, and alienated from his former self and his society.

In any case, he certainly does not seem to be the sort of man who could bring to this spectacular woman the intellectual challenge and emotional commitment she expected in a husband. He seems to have given his second wife some brief moments of happiness before he turned permanently to anger and alcohol. At least one friend noted that she assumed he was a marginal mental case, who perhaps should have been institutionalized. Eric Whelpton, Sayers' friend from Oxford and France, said that she confided to him that her husband was "awful."[15] Other friends were inclined to agree.

Dorothy L. Sayers, who wisely kept her maiden name for her writing, never left Fleming. Biographers insist that she was miserably unhappy with him much of the time, but she supported the household and paid his pub bills until his death—shortly before her own.

Aside from his daughter, those inclined to present the Fleming side of the case note that he was, in spite of his years, far more attractive and personable in the eyes of the world than his dowdy wife. He is said to have been a better cook than she, a better photographer, and a good artist. His daughter cannot accept the premise that he never earned a living after his second marriage. She suspects he hid his income to avoid alimony payments, providing us with an unattractive choice between thinking him incompetent and thinking him dishonest. Sayers herself was always close about money, but the evidence suggests she was absolutely scrupulous in business dealings. For example, she refused to take more money from the BBC than her contract called for, despite the enormous overage on time and trouble in her writing of *The Man Born to Be King*. Anyone who adhered this strictly to a contractual agreement would be unlikely to countenance her husband's cheating on tax and alimony by hiding his income.

On the contrary, she appears to have sought out occasions to praise him, and she was painfully aware of his sensitivity about her superior earning power. Her novels henceforth chronicle grotesque arguments between lovers and spouses over the woman's earnings. The greater likelihood is that, once freed of the necessity of writing in order to eat, he gave less time to the typewriter and more to the bottle. A strong woman can disminish a man's independence and self-esteem by her very competence. Rather than challenging him to adopt her fast pace of achievement and become her comrade on the great adventure of life, she can take over his responsibilities and unman him, unintentionally reducing him to childish reliance on her. The fault may well have been his; Sayers loved a good fight. But poor Mac may have been too worn out to be a good opponent and may have preferred a peevish defeat. She was not the sort of person who could pull her punches with someone she considered her equal. Even a friend as close to her as Dr. Reynolds notes that she often overwhelmed her in argument, noting afterward that if her opponent insisted on handing her a hammer, she should not be criticized for using it. The sad possibility is that Dorothy Sayers met Fleming when she was at the peak of her physical and intellectual vigor, and when he was too old and too tired and too hurt to be an equal partner for her. He seems to have resented her and her work, growing petty and querulous and demanding, greeting her return from a triumphal speech with a complaint that she had not fixed his dinner on time. She told one friend that he even sneered at her work on Dante, forcing her to work when he was out of the house. But Sayers' public references to him are warm and affectionate.

Whatever the dynamics of the Fleming-Sayers household, it is obvious from her work that this tragic mistake of the wrong marriage brought Dorothy Sayers perilously close to Doubting Castle and to the confrontation with Giant Despair. By all odds, it was the lowest point in her life, more painful to a woman who had such great visions of what love and marriage can be. It was a nadir that continued for years and was reflected in numerous books.

Lord Peter echoes his maker's depression. Though he bounces through the opening pages of *The Unpleasantness at the Bellona Club* with much of his old manner, he soon finds his jokes turned sour and his views darkened. The flippancy of the opening is mirrored in the comic discovery of the murder victim, a literal reenactment of the Old *Punch* joke: " 'Take him away!' said Fentiman, 'take him away. He's been dead two days!' "[16] The lighthearted manner in which Lord Peter discovers the corpse in the chair at the Bellona Club reminds us of the nude body in the bathtub of the first novel. The effort to investigate the death without disturbing the lethal tranquillity of the club produces a delightful commentary on stuffy British traditions that ignore violence and sin. The proper society will seek to maintain its surface calm at any price, with even old war veterans considering murder an "unpleasant" nuisance.

The brittle tone of intellectualism and wit and indifference is damaged by Lord Peter's visit to his old friend George, the deceased man's grandson and heir. The painful effects of shell shock and George's disintegrating marriage with Sheila (his patient-Griselda wife) bring Peter back to his own war memories. Like Dorothy Sayers, Lord Peter had gone through a nervous breakdown. Sayers had reason to understand the effect on a nervous person of a shell-shock victim. Lord Peter's sympathy exacerbates his own old pain and brings him to the edge of the chaotic nightmare world he had himself escaped. Certainly her husband's war nerves must have recalled Sayers' adolescent bout with mental distress. The first stage in responding to the disorder in another's mind is belief and sympathy. Following the convolutions of mental illness can be so exhausting as to disorient the healthy mind. This of course would be even worse in a case where the sympathy was mingled with love.

Lord Peter discovers the gradual need to pull away from his friend and become more objective and dispassionate before he can be of any real help. Gradually, he analyzes George and Shelia's needs, organizes their flat, and helps solve the mystery. The solutions are to be found in common sense and practical activity. But even with all his practical wisdom, Lord Peter finds himself deeply disturbed by the experience. He has grown too sympathetic with the murder suspect and finds therefore that the search for truth is clouded. The discovery of the solution does not always lead the detective into an experience of joy. The deepening of Lord Peter's active involvement with his suspects, and the growing complexity of his responses, hint at his increasing need for a deeper satisfaction in human relationships that will not find resolution for some years and several novels. *Bellona Club* lacks the pat conclusions of Sayers' earliest work, leaving a number of unanswered questions about human relationships.

The painful picture of the Fentiman marriage is too realistic in the story to be either funny or entirely fictional. George Fentiman—in frequent pain as a result of gassing, in constant torment because of his shattered nerves, angry at his good wife's compassion and self-possession (and probably puzzled at his own behavior with the woman he loves), unable to hold a job, inclined to drink too much, to fall into inexplicable fits of fury, to incoherence and self-loathing and remorse—George is no comic portrait. In another age he would have been labeled "demon-ridden." But in the postwar, enlightened era, he was diagnosed as shell-shocked and incurable. Poor Sheila, his harried wife, finds no romance in her life or pleasure in her work. George resents the bad meals and the dirty flat, but makes no move to do anything to rectify the situation. To him, housework is woman's work and breadwinning is man's. Sheila's unwilling role as sole support of the family places her in a position of economic superiority. Her husband paranoically spies in her innocent speeches—though they are occasionally laced with self-pity—evidence of arrogance and disdain for him. He ascribes resentment to her even when she neither expresses nor hints at it. While disapproving of her work, he is forced grudgingly to accept her money and then orders her about the house to reassert his dominant masculinity. She finds him a constant worry, a nag, a bully, and a drunk.

All of the women in the novel are hungry for love. Marjorie Phelps, for example, Peter's good friend, is an intelligent and self-sufficient artist who moves from one unsatisfying affair to another. " 'People have a perfect right to want love-affairs,' " she asserts defensively, in the tone of the "new" liberated woman.[17] Unwilling to accept the Victorian notion of arranged marriages, or adjust to their role as lonely spinsters (in the Climpson mode), the women grope for love in undignified and painful ways. The men, knowing this, may use the women's sexual and emotional hunger for their own purposes, playing with their needs. The sickening portrait emerges of the male as self-loathing and self-justifying and parasitic.

Dorothy L. Sayers came closer in *Bellona Club* than ever before to accepting the notion of the battle of the sexes. The old world was as dead as the corpse in the chair at the club, but the new one was still waiting to be born. There were plenty of new women around, but not enough new men for real companionship. Lord Peter finds pleasure in independent, intelligent women, but most men cannot accept the new woman.

Near the end of the novel, Lord Peter advises a distraught, plain young woman that she will need to accept the dominant role in love, for hers will be the "leading brain of the two." He comments that she should marry a "man of the world" who can appreciate her aging like a fine wine.[18] Unfortunately, men are not inclined to see a substantial woman with a well-stocked mind as a vintage *Romanee Conti* so much as an overripe fruit. One of Lord Peter's advantages is that he can voice opinions which, coming from a man of the world, seem sensitive and perceptive. The same comments expressed in the voice of a fat middle-aged woman would appear self-serving. If Ann Dorland, the object of Peter's concern, finds the right man, that lover will delight in her superiority, and the two will make a good marriage based on mutual esteem. But such a promise is only hinted in this novel, when Major Fentiman appears, at the conclusion, to be developing some appreciation of her good qualities—her courage, generosity, decency, femininity, and sweet nature. He tells Lord Peter that it is " 'about time somebody brought a little brightness into that poor girl's life.' "[19] He asserts that he is planning to undertake this task, perhaps a touch of hope in a novel which, for the most part, ends with frustration, upheaval, and dissatisfaction.

The "Chelsea women" in the story are for the most part physically unattractive and emotionally starved. They are deeply embarrassed at their own sexual appetites, and humiliated in their relationships with exploitive men. Lord Peter is a refreshing breath in this sordid atmosphere: he refuses to leap casually into the nearest bed, laughs at pornography, and denies the mastery of the glands. Though he can sympathize with the various women, he is not ready to confuse that sympathy with love and suggest marriage. In fact, no perfect mate yet looms on his horizon. All of these humiliating sexual experiences will perforce end in imperfect alliances. The Fentimans will stay together, continue their fruitless quarrels; needing one another, hurting one another, and in their own way loving one another. Sayers seems to think, for the moment, that this is the sum total of the possible in this imperfect world. Yet Peter says of the angry and pitiful and warped husband of this marriage, " 'I like old George. He's an awful pig in some ways, but I quite like him.' "[20] The reason for the liking is not apparent in the story, unless it is sympathy and identification, but the affection is real. We might well assume that such an irrational affection—along with her firm Anglo-Catholic antagonism to divorce—kept Sayers faithful to a similar pitiful tyrant in her own imperfect union.

The book is one of Sayers' darkest, undoubtedly reflecting the mood of disappointment in her own life. Biographers are still seeking to unravel the torment of these days, but, as she notes in the novel, women are not inclined to tell other women much about their sexual disasters. We do know this: Dorothy L. Sayers married in 1926, and by 1928 the novels clearly reflect her newly developed and painfully expressed notion of marriage-as-hostility.

The next novel, *The Documents in the Case*, co-authored with Robert Eustace (a pseudonym for Eustace Robert Barton, M.D.) and published in 1930, continues this same image of marriage as a prison for two. Again the petty, nagging husband chides his wife on her advanced ideas and her failure in her own proper role. Again the peevish arguments dodge, weave, and circle back, making solution impossible and logic irrelevant. Again the confrontations are public and embarrassing. And this time they lead to violence.

In the period between these novels, Sayers was more successful and productive than ever. She had brought out a collection of short stories, *Lord Peter Views the Body*, and her first *Omnibus of Crime* with its brilliant introduction. She had enough money to enlarge and refurbish her Bloomsbury flat and to buy a small home in Witham, a village in Essex outside London. She also had the opportunity to do the first scholarly production since she left Oxford, her translation of Thomas's medieval fragment *Tristan in Brittany*—a story of lust and marriage and adultery and violence (subjects much on her mind). The introductory comments by the famous scholar George Saintsbury pay well-deserved tribute to this versatile woman. She continued to maintain her interest in scholarship, writing articles for the journal of the Modern Language Association, and later serving as the president of that association for six years.

Her flat in Bloomsbury was close enough to the British Museum to encourage her visits there to study the twelfth-century manuscript of the Norman poet Thomas. Her continuing cultivation of scholarly habits, even when her life was full of emotional turmoil, suggests a true love of learning and of the peaceful life of the intellect. Certainly she must have stolen the time. Her publisher recalls that he had to meet her for business discussions after she came from work at Benson's in the evening. With her heavy writing schedule, her regular working hours, and her home responsibilities, she could hardly have had much time for scholarly research among the manuscripts of the British Museum. But her frenetic schedule also left little time for the futile contemplation of her irrevocable errors. She may have sought solace in activity.

In the midst of all of this growth in prosperity and activity and reputation, she lost the two people she had counted on most in her life. First her father died and then her mother. During the brief period of her mother's widowhood, Sayers brought her to live at the house in Witham. Then, at her death, she buried her mother beside her father at Christchurch. She allowed no solemn hymns at their funerals and raised no monuments to them. She knew full well that death had no victory over these remarkable Christian folk. In *The Nine Tailors*, written six years later, she paid tribute to them, their marriage, their ministry, and their tastes. In some ways, that book was to be her monument to her parents; in another sense, she knew that she herself, their only child, must be their living monument. But without their support and comfort in her life, her mood darkened and her output of work reached a frenzied pace.

In 1930, she was able to publish a prodigious load of work: *The Documents in the Case*, *Strong Poison*, and a number of articles on detective fiction. By the following year, she was financially independent and able at last to leave the job at Benson's. She may have thought that the change of pace and residence would help the marriage, and she had promised herself from the beginning that the advertising work was only a temporary expedient. So, after nine years at her "temporary" work, she moved with her husband and maiden aunt to Witham, settling into the home made possible, in part, by her father's final bequest. She retained the flat on Great James Street, dividing her time between London and the village for the rest of her life.[21]

Her small row house (which was actually two adjoining cottages with a common front added in the eighteenth century) on a busy street in this Essex village was important to her. She could walk or cycle to the train station and take a train to London, arriving there within the hour. But she could at the same time enjoy the ambience of the village: take an active part in the life of the fourteenth-century parish church, order her special herbs from the local greengrocer, walk out at night and chat with the local doctor, stop to watch a plumber at work on the street. She could laugh at her aunt's parrot, watch her cat, or ridicule her pig; she could work in her garden, share sherry with a neighbor, sit before the fire with Mac and knit stockings, and then disappear into her study to read and to think and to write. The move took her away from the noisy and faceless existence of the great brown city with its blackened buildings and endless queues. She now passed green pastures and tree-lined streams to live among the folk who maintained a sense of order and individuality so precious to her.

But even the village has it pubs and its temptations, and life appears to have gone on in a steadily painful pattern. As time went on, Dorothy Sayers apparently came to see her husband less as a lover and more as a responsibility. (She once noted that the pleasure of the detective story was that it posed a problem that could be solved and provided the materials for that solution. Unfortunately, her life did not follow such a tidy pattern.) Whether she wished to or not, she seems not to have brought her son Anthony into their home, though he did take Fleming's name. He stayed with her cousin Ivy Shrimpton during his early years. Dorothy Sayers visited Anthony regularly, sending him letters and presents. Later she sent him to boarding schools, and finally to Oxford. But he never became a significant part of her day-to-day life and was never legally adopted.

This sad marriage apparently had no room for children. Fleming's daughter, as noted earlier, believed that Dorothy Sayers forbade his children to visit. Biographers suspect that Fleming refused to allow Anthony to live with them. In brief, their relationship seems to have become cruelly possessive and mutually tormenting, excluding all others. They may have been too old and set in their ways to enjoy children with their noise, chatter, and emotional demands. Their ages at the time of marriage and their individual life-styles may have ruled out any interest in building a family. For whatever reasons, they seem to have settled for their mismatched *ménage à deux*. One cynic summarizes their marriage this way: "he drank; she ate."

In a long letter she wrote to Reverend Aubrey Moody when he was preparing to be a priest, she commented that she was less ready to generalize about divorce than marriage:

> I could deliver a few heart-felt sentiments about certain things which make some people almost impossible to live with, such as jealousy and possessiveness and habitual discourtesy—or about the preposterous emphasis laid nowadays on the importance of one's 'love-life'; what with novels and film and Freudian psychology and what-not, you can hardly blame people for thinking that failure in that is failure in everything—though half the time that isn't true at all; it's only that there is an almost insupportable pressure on people to think so.[22]

She apparently found a way to resist this pressure, and to accept defeat as final.

With her parents gone, her son at school, and her husband deteriorating into alcoholism, she must have been a very lonely person. Her writing and her friendship with an increasingly wide range of people became an antidote for her pain. The Christian path never ends with tragedy. It goes through the pain, beyond the cross to the resurrection. Gradually the darkness began to lift from her life, and she started the experience of renewal.

IV. Pilgrim of the Heart

Lord Peter helped Dorothy Sayers in her recovery. He paid her bills and freed her from Benson's and he took her on a journey back into her life, allowing her to meditate on her experience from his perspective. The next decade of her life saw Sayers becoming increasingly mellow and comfortable with her success and her opportunities. This resilience was apparently founded on no dramatic change in her life, no dynamic lover who swept her off her feet (wool stockings and brogans included), no dramatic conversion experience with public confessions of her dark past. Rather, she set to work in her usual way to make something of the life she had been given. She once said, in talking about the difference between the artist and the average person, that the artist is living in the "way of grace." This is not to say that artists handle personal life especially well, but that they are using their lives to "make something new." As a result of this, "the pains and sorrows of this troublesome world can never, for [the artist] . . . , be *wholly* meaningless and useless, as they are to the man who dumbly endures them and can . . . 'make nothing of them.' " Dealing in a creative way with our problems is to make something of them, even when they are "insoluble."[1]

At least four of her novels, and in part many others, deal with

Sayers' problems in quite special ways. These novels are all based on particular places she had lived, people she had known, and ideas that derived from those circumstances. They comprise some of her most interesting mature considerations on her life and her friends.

The Five Red Herrings pictures the landscape around Galloway where the Flemings enjoyed vacations among the fisherfolk and the art community. It provides an opportunity for Sayers to classify kinds of artists, problems they have with one another and their families, and the patterns of their lives. In this story, remembering pleasant times that she and her husband shared among other artists and fisherfolk, Sayers acknowledges the jealousy, egocentricity, extreme anger, and pettiness that appear to be part of the artist's life. She came to know men so late in life that she expected too much of them; it is a comfort of sorts to see that most bohemians are not beautiful people, but folk plagued with problems attendant on the creative life. People who rely on a talent need strict isolation, but afterward they hope for pleasure in public reception of their art. Small criticisms can trigger passionate reactions. And furthermore, artists, because they are by nature "loners," find that even those they love become a burden and an irritant from time to time. One painter in the book is so tantalized by the lure of the free life that he even leaves the wife he deeply loves to earn his way in the medieval craft pattern, as a wandering painter of tavern signs. In the book, Sayers enters the various homes, shows the stresses and distresses of living with creative people, and discovers that marriage is not usually—and probably should not be expected to be—the source of all human happiness. The creative people find their greatest joy in their work.

Two years later, in 1933 (when she was forty years old and had been away from Benson's for three years), she wrote her realistic study of the advertising business. Though the value judgments are now clear and she has acknowledged that advertising is not the work for her, she does portray the fun of the business, the wit of its people, and the pressures they must expect. She can laugh now at the archetypal English housewife the copywriter seeks to motivate, and at the foolishness of the values touted. The economic problems that disturbed her were to reappear in later essays; the contemporary values also found their places in her later writings. She discovered that her years at the agency gave her important insights into the problems of her world. She had not been wasting her time during those ten years at Benson's. She had been storing up her mind for her real work.

The following year, she published *The Nine Tailors*, her tribute to her father and mother and to the folk of the fen country. In retrospect, she discovered she enjoyed among these folk the same joy she found in her medieval studies, a realism and bluntness, and awareness of the enduring values, and a capacity for survival. They formed an island of peace after the sophisticates of London and the intelligentsia of bohemia. She was to discover that they were her real audience and her real subject.

For most Lord Peter enthusiasts, the book that moved them most strongly was her Oxford novel, *Gaudy Night*. It was also the work that drew most heavily on her own experiences and intellectual ideals. It came after her return to Oxford as a guest speaker at a Gaudy Night celebration, and it helped her to understand why her path had moved so far from scholarship into a world so different from what she had anticipated. It also gave her the chance to consider what love should be between man and woman. If she could not have the experience in her life, she could certainly have it in her creative imagination.

In order to write of love in *Gaudy Night*, Sayers had had to establish the proper woman for Lord Peter and bring her through a series of novels, developing and understanding her so that their courtship and marriage would be more than a fictitious romantic interlude. For this, she needed to create Harriet D. Vane.

In *Strong Poison* (1930), Lord Peter met his destiny—the accused murderer of her lover. He watches her as she stands (like his brother) accused of a crime she insists she did not commit, while (unlike his brother) courageously conceding the illicit behavior for which the society does indeed condemn her. She is not pretty, with her square eyebrows and smudged eyes; but she has considerable appeal for Lord Peter. He admires her strength in adversity, her wit in pain, her wisdom about people in spite of her foolish past errors. Right now, she is not so vivacious as we might expect of his intended, but she has had the fun knocked out of her by a bullying lover who first pressured her into an illicit arrangement and who then humiliated her by offering to reward her bad behavior with marriage. She feels manipulated and used by him, but not to the point that she is willing to murder him. Her distress clouds her judgment and keeps her from being the best investigator of her own case.

She is a detective-story writer, a very good one. In fact, her success was a bone of contention with her lover, who insisted he was a better writer despite his lack of popular success. She is a doctor's daughter, from a small village, became an Oxford scholar, taking a first in her examinations, and won her M.A. in languages from "Shrewsbury" College. Sayers gives Harriet Vane her own distaste for makeup, except for some powder, her own disregard for clothing, except elaborate costumes on special occasions. She too loves cigarettes and her tea time. Though she has much in common with Sayers, she has more physical beauty, more opportunities for romance, and eventually a more comfortable life than Sayers. She does not, however, accomplish nearly so much.

But Lord Peter thinks she would make an interesting wife, a woman whom he could enjoy knowing and with whom he could discuss ideas, one who would tell him the truth. She would be a partner able to share his life and to enrich it. Harriet, however, having been hurt more recently than Peter, is less sanguine about any lasting relationship. As an expression of her gratitude for his help in clearing her of the crime, she offers to live with him, but not to marry him. Without realizing that she is inflicting the same pain on him that her dead lover Philip inflicted on her, she dully confesses that she feels nothing. Her bitterness in discovering that she has embarrassed her family and ruined her reputation for the sake of a cad leaves her too damaged to feel either love or lust. Lord Peter will have to bide patiently the right moment for her renewal of spirit.

The book is full of cultured people who view human relationships as a meaningless game. The lawyers treat the trial as a game of wits, the murderer treats the victim as the other player in a game of death, and the press treat the whole trial as a circus for their entertainment and use. The humanity of our old friends—Lord Peter, Parker, Miss Climpson, Marjorie Phelps, and the Dowager Duchess—contrasts refreshingly with the common pattern of manipulating pawns. Lord Peter, who sets out not to win a case but to discover the truth about a woman he admires and to help her preserve and reconstruct her life, does not demand payment in servility. Having freed her of the murder charge, he refuses to press his advantages. He can admire and protect another person's talent and independence. He is seeking a friend, not a worshiper or a victim. At the end, he slips off unthanked. He thereby forces Harriet to sense the incompleteness of the action and her own cruelty.

The career woman, Sayers had discovered, had a constant battle with convention. Although she might appear to be justified in working so long as she needs the money, she finds constant and unrelenting opposition if she works for pleasure. So long as Harriet is single, this is less of a problem, though some would judge her adversely for refusing to live the traditional spinster life as the shadow in the family home, serving as an upper servant, self-effacing and supernumerary. Certainly, a career would seem preferable to the older pattern, but only so long as it is not the woman's primary concern. Her eye must still be on the ultimate target—an eligible male. In having Harriet refuse the repeated proposals of the wealthy and desirable Lord Peter, she must have shocked many in her audience. She was establishing her heroine as a career woman who loved her work and found meaning in it. Even when Harriet finally agrees to the marriage, she does not relinquish her work; nor does Lord Peter wish her to do so. He certainly does not expect to relinquish his and would never ask another to make a sacrifice to *his* ego, especially a sacrifice he would not be willing to make himself. (The D. in Harriet's name is for Deborah, the warrior-judge who is the most unfeminine woman in the Old Testament.)

The next Harriet D. Vane novel, published in 1932, was *Have His Carcase*. In this story, Harriet has collected herself from the shock of brutalizing love, has set a new course for her life, and has begun to look about her. She is still hurt, but obviously healing. Though she notes the condescending attitudes of men, she does not insist on feminist confrontations. Laughing inwardly at common stereotypes of manliness and womanliness, she plays by society's rules, manipulating the blind believers in her own game. She brazenly announces her reputation, while privately aching at the response and the necessity. Increasingly, we see her as a double personality, one for the gross and insensitive public, the other for loving and sympathetic friends. In her bitterness, she sees this role-playing not as a duplicity but as the plan for survival.

Sayers uses clothing as a symbol of this manipulation of roles: when Harriet is most herself, she wears walking shoes and sensible clothes; Peter likes her in these. When she seeks to please him, she buys a dress that Peter suggests would enhance her natural color, thereby flattering him by her consideration of his tastes. When she is least herself, she dresses as a parody of fluttering and uncomfortable womanliness. This delights the "manly" man but dismays Lord Peter, who immediately dubs the frilly and exaggerated outfit "ridiculous." He does not demand that she act a part for him; he enjoys her most when she is most fully herself. His love is not a trap but a liberation of the real woman within. Later, in *Gaudy Night*, Harriet has become more clothes-conscious and more eager to please both Peter and herself. But she never bows down to worship at the shrine of "St. Henna," the patron saint of those grotesque matrons at the watering place who seek to compensate for fading beauty with ever heavier makeup and ever younger clothing. She prefers to grow old with grace. (Sayers sees thirty as "old.") Their pursuit of sleek young gigolos is the inevitable conclusion to their constant denigration of self. Harriet sees in them the cult of youth that denies the values of maturity. The real Fountain of Youth is not in this run-down watering place but in the creative imagination.

The hero and heroine, by contrast to the game-players of the story, discover in their relationship a maturing friendship based on harmony of interests, mutual respect, honesty (to the point of embarrassment), and laughter. Harriet can look frankly at Peter's body in a swimsuit and admire the shoulders and the calves, an ironic reversal of the many feminine breasts and legs scrutinized by heroes in other stories. Lord Peter, for his part, refuses to comment on her appearance except in extreme circumstances. He does not pick her apart as a catalogue of goodies for his aesthetic pleasure, for he sees her as a total person. When he does praise her, it is for her shrewdness and her wit, those characteristics she herself cherishes. Considerate of painful zones in her damaged psyche, he is gentle and sensitive to her needs. He waits quietly for her to come to him, standing ready with his declarations of love, and his light acceptance of her preferences for independence. He is waiting for her to heal.

In her effort at reconstruction, Harriet must grow "vain" or at least self-confident again, not about her talent, which she never doubted, but about her womanliness. And then she has to be able to feel concern for another person, caring more about him and his needs than about herself and hers. When she suddenly perceives the full intelligence, wit, courtesy, wealth, education, and charm of Lord Peter (the qualities of the medieval lover), she is "crushed" with a sense of her inferiority. That she can learn to delight in this "godlike" man at the price of her own egotism is testimony to her new health.[2] Lord Peter is to Harriet what Beatrice is to Dante—a God-bearer who restores her faith in human nature and sets her back on the path to salvation.

The growing oneness of man and woman allows each to become more fully human. Peter becomes less silly, more richly emotional and complex. Harriet becomes less wooden, more charming and joyful. They seek no stereotypes of manliness and womanliness, they make no demands of subjection and sacrifice. They simply enjoy, encourage, and grow individually and together. Having discovered that she need not rely on a man, Harriet can enjoy the thrill of freely leaning toward Peter in a delicate balance. Rather than snatching happiness for the moment, they build a lasting happiness that will deepen with age. The book ends appropriately with the two returning "home"—leaving the trivial vanities of the watering place for their life of the mind and spirit.

Sayers had argued against the use of women detectives in her introduction to the first *Omnibus of Crime*, saying that "they are obliged to be so irritatingly intuitive as to destroy that quiet enjoyment of the logical which we look for in our detective reading.[3] This, of course, she reversed by making Harriet even more logical than Lord Peter, so much so that she misses the more obvious emotional point in some cases, especially in *Gaudy Night*. The other extreme of the liberated woman detective, the woman-as-hero, bothered Sayers in still another way, for such a woman insists "on walking into physical danger and hampering the men engaged on the job." They are altogether too "active and courageous" for real life. The specter of marriage "looms too large in their view of life"—not an especially surprising circumstance, since they are invariably "young and beautiful."[4] Her own heroine seldom dabbled in real danger if she could avoid it. Harriet is no courageous, vigorous sleuth. She is at best an amateur, who has crime thrust upon her. She does not seek it out; but when confronted with it, she turns a cool, analytic mind to it—and at last calls Lord Peter.

The turning to Peter occurs in *Gaudy Night*. She had accepted his help with poor grace in *Strong Poison*, and accepted his presence with delight in *Have His Carcase*, and finally asks him to help her in *Gaudy Night*. When she can acknowledge weakness, she no longer worries about her own strength, and she is ready for love. Dorothy L. Sayers admitted that Harriet was not the only one who needed reformation. She says that she worked for three "longish books" to humanize Peter for Harriet, who was already human.[5] He was, in fact, becoming too human to serve her purpose as a detective. Her decision was to let him go his own free way, marry Harriet, and die off as a detective. She had also decided that Harriet must come to Peter as a "free agent," one who respected her own independence before she could bring him her "dependence as a willing gift." In Eliot's words, he must avoid, at all costs, demanding that she commit "the greatest treason;/To do the right deed for the wrong reason."[6] Ordinarily, Sayers thought the mingling of love and detection to be unwise. Love interest, in a detective story, is only justified when central to the plot; most often, however, it is dragged in as an irrelevance. Certainly no relationship between crime-plot and love-plot could be more organic than the one in *Gaudy Night*.

Sayers had originally planned a "straight novel" about professional women.[7] The idea was to use as her heroine a woman graduate of Oxford who found, "in middle life, and after a reasonably satisfactory experience of marriage and motherhood, that her real vocation and full emotional fulfilment were to be found in the creative life of the intellect."[8] But, when she considered the characters she had already at hand, their natures and obvious paths, she could not reject their need to meet in this still center of the intellect which is their "home." The return to Oxford for the "Gaudy" convinced her that Harriet, who stood equal with Peter on the intellectual platform, must meet him here. "In that sphere she had never been false to her own standards."[9]

In her fascinating essay on *Gaudy Night*, Sayers acknowledged that both Peter and Harriet are extensions of facets of herself. Aside from the accidental attributes they need because of their roles in the novels, they are essentially complements of one another, intended for union. Peter "is seen to be the familiar figure of the interpretative artist, the romantic soul at war with the realistic brain." And, on the other side, Harriet "with her lively and inquisitive mind and her soul grounded upon reality, is his complement—the creative artist."[10]

One of the loveliest images in the story, which helps develop and explain Sayers' notion of human love, is music. When they stand in the antique shop and sing together, they discover their common delight in polyphony. " 'Anybody can have harmony,' " Peter tells Harriet, " 'if they will leave us the counterpoint.' "[11] Their shared knowledge of music allows them to delight in a coded conversation full of subtle references to various songs—principally from the seventeenth century. And at the end of the story, they sit together in their unisex academic gowns, listening to the duet played by two masters. To play a successful duet, the artists must be more than fiddlers, they must be musicians. Such is also true of the delicate balance Sayers sought in the duet of marriage. This duet finds its full development in the sequel to *Gaudy Night*, the final Lord Peter Wimsey novel, *Busman's Honeymoon.*

Dorothy L. Sayers waited a while to marry off her lovers. She wrote the honeymoon story first as a play and then as a novel, blending their experience of love with another story of violence, and lacing it with her own taste for Elizabethan love lyrics. In some ways, it is her most erotic published work (although the unpublished *Thrones, Dominations* takes it a step further), and at the same time her most theological one. Since it was written at a time she was becoming a popular Christian apologist, called to be a public speaker, becoming a radio personality, and soon to be a writer of chancel drama, this religious tone is to be expected.

The actual surface story of *Busman's Honeymoon* is the marriage and honeymoon of Harriet and Peter. They purchase a country home near the village where Harriet lived as a girl and spend their honeymoon in it. They find that the house is haunted by the life of the mean old man who owned and abused it, and who was finally murdered in it. They must empty and exorcise it before they can make it their own. But in a sense, home is not in a house for them, but in one another's hearts.

Dorothy L. Sayers had been very reluctant to make specific religious statements in her novels. She did have her characters discuss the basic argument between science and religion in her collaborative effort, *The Documents in the Case*. And the women in *Gaudy Night* argue the merits of the disinterested intellect. The forthright attack on capitalistic exploitation in *Murder Must Advertise* went about as far as she was willing to go in explicit social commentary. But on the topic of religion, she allows little explicit statement.

From beginning to end, Lord Peter shows scant enthusiasm for religious ecstasy. Though one of the Wimseys had been a martyr under old Queen Mary, martyrdom and sainthood were not characteristic family traits. Rather, Sayers presents her hero as " 'an eighteenth-century Whig gentleman, born a little out of his time, and doubtful whether any claim to possess a soul is not a rather vulgar piece of presumption.' "[12] The aristocratic Lord Peter prefers to concern himself with morality—his responsibility to his fellow creatures. Though we see him at church, he feels the need to justify his attendance as a social obligation rather than a religious commitment. When called upon to read the Old Testament lesson, he does so with attention to his audience (including a bad little boy who is pinching his sister) and his own recent activities. Jeremiah neatly justifies Peter's own service to the cause of justice.

In *The Nine Tailors*, set so centrally in the house of God, Lord Peter comes close to a religious experience. But to discuss the sense of God's power and majesty in public would be as embarrassing to him as discussing the details of his toilet. It is simply not done in polite company. And Dorothy L. Sayers will not make a puppet of her free character, forcing him to mouth sentiments contrary to his nature or his sense of decorum. Miss Climpson can discuss the thrills of the faith because she is an effusive old maid. The urbane gentleman must prepare his mask for his public, much as the almost imperturbable Bunter must do.

The more subtle and personal ritual for him is that of his work—his form of worship. He feels called by his natural abilities, his native inquisitiveness, analytic talents, and God-given wits, to seek out malefactors and (usually) bring them to the bar of justice. Knowing that all have sinned and fallen short of the glory of God, he acknowledges that the motive for violence is widespread. But between the thought and the act lies a great gulf—determining a social creature on the one hand and a criminal on the other. The unpunished murderer grows arrogant and kills again. Society, he assures us several times, is not safe without the punishment of guilt.

Yet the agent of revelation—and consequent punishment—cannot be puffed up with his own virtue. The motive for pursuit of truth can be almost as clouded as the motive for crime. Fortune falls without precise justice. Thus an unhappy and poor young man, running an affair with one local girl and a courtship with an older spinster, cannot be judged by quite the same standards as a wealthy lord and his jubilant bride. Their happiness, though long awaited, is neither inevitable nor earned. If each of us had perfect justice, who would escape?

This is the reason that Harriet hates to implicate the poor spinster in her uncle's death and the reason Peter seeks to comfort the murderer. After trapping the man into a confession, Lord Peter seeks counsel for him, arranges for his lover in her pregnancy, and begs his forgiveness. But the unrepentant murderer dies unforgiving while the distraught Peter weeps for himself and for the soul of the damned man.

This ritual apparently is repeated in some form with each execution. Over and over Lord Peter acknowledges the dubious fruit of his actions and seeks human forgiveness.

Only in this pattern and in his love for Harriet does he show the sensitivity of his inner core, which is usually shielded by his brittle veneer. The perfect detective would hide this; thus, the increasingly obvious intensity and anguish of Lord Peter point to his demise as a perfect detective and his birth as an ideal father. Though created as a tool for expressing his author's rapier wit and traditional wisdom, he becomes his own man. *Busman's Honeymoon* is a curious final Wimsey mystery: it starts (like the first one, *Whose Body?*) in the light tone of a comedy of manners, but ends with the cathartic tragic experience of death and cleansing tears.

Hidden beneath the neat Elizabethan framework of the novel—a fitting instrument on which to collaborate with Muriel St. Clare Byrne, an Elizabethan scholar—is a subtle system of religious symbolism that adumbrates the chancel drama written shortly after. The book appears to be exactly what it is advertised: a love story with detective intrusions. Certainly it is a celebration of married love, as opposed to the study of illicit love in *Tristan*. It is the physical and spiritual merging of two human lights into a single brilliant flame, a tribute to the metaphysics of love so beautifully articulated by John Donne.

It is also an affirmation of life and human love as a path toward God. When Peter asks his wife whether she thinks life " 'good on the whole,' " she asserts her delight in human existence. " 'Yes! I've always felt absolutely certain it was good.' "[13] Though plagued with troubles and threatened with death, she never thought of taking her own life. Life itself, even on these painful terms, is good.

Yet, making life complete and thrilling demands a "miracle"—an experience that gives every moment new meaning. In Scripture, this is the "breath of life" breathed into the dead matter, the water turned suddenly into wine. For Harriet, the earthly paradise lies in Peter's arms. She finds in him her "God-bearer." For her, he turns the water of life into fine wine. Lust becomes love at the miracle of his touch. In this miracle of love, the humbled Peter finds himself amazed: "as though somebody had credited him with the possession of a soul."[14] Their shared ecstasy becomes a liberation for them, a new birth into a new freedom. Their language sounds like Dante's as he meets his Beatrice in the Earthly Paradise: they too speak of the miter and the crown. In their love, they become for themselves bishop and king, needing no authority outside of love. They need fear no vows of obedience, because they are one flesh and spirit. Neither seeks to dominate or condescend. They need not seek forgiveness, for they have canceled out all debts in their baptism of love, remembering only the experience of joy. They no longer pursue one another like the frenzied lovers in Dante's Hell, because—like Augustine—they have found their rest in love.

In her notes on Dante and Charles Williams—the scholar-friend who led her to find joy in her faith—she explained the difference between happiness and joy, a significant Christian differentiation. While happiness usually is a term applied to a life of good fortune and contented disposition, and is usually the assessment of a person's total career, joy is very different. In fact, she notes, people of a happy temperament are seldom capable of joy because they are insufficiently sensitive. "Joy (except for those saints who live continually in the presence of God) is of its nature brief and almost instantaneous." It is, she says, "an apprehension of the eternal moment."[15] And in the ecstasy, joy breaks open the very gates of hell. Sayers, like C. S. Lewis, in the middle of her life, was surprised by joy.

Harriet and Lord Peter in their love found renewal. Peter's dream of chained men (who sound like Eliot's hollow men in the cactus land) ends with Harriet and a dream of chrysanthemums—a new life out of the old enslavement. She, like God—and the virgin Mary, in this medieval symbolism—waits for a chosen man to seek her out, and then welcomes him to joy and peace.

Dorothy L. Sayers never made public her own experience of human love or divine. She instead gave us the universal experience through Harriet and Peter, and remained silent about the facts of her individual path. In her dedication-letter to *Busman's Honeymoon*, she notes the joys of friendship, and in her essays she speaks of the thrilling experience of God in life, but she invariably shut the door to any private inquiry. She may easily have gained her knowledge of ideal human love from her favorite seventeenth-century poets, who had brilliantly expressed the ideal for the Christian lover.

As part of her Way of Affirmation, the acceptance of this world and its images as the first step on the path toward God, Sayers uses sexuality as an image of union with the divine. She brings the Elizabethan equating of sexual union with physical death to bear on the book, so that the epithalamion is interrupted by murder. The presence of death in life increases the very preciousness of life itself. While arid lust makes a wasteland of human experience, their fertile love looks forward to children, to renewal. Their right use of the body and the spirit "sweetens the atmosphere" of the house haunted by its wretched old miserly owner. Their joy exorcises his wrath. Like Eliot, who had seen a world hungry for meaning and longing for fertility, Dorothy L. Sayers saw it eager for love and redemption, open to the experience of joy.

Though Harriet and Lord Peter were to reappear with their sons in stories of domestic tranquillity for some time, writing letters of advice in time of war, and suggesting proper patterns for child-raising, they were in fact complete. Having found paradise, they had nowhere else to go. As Peter tells Harriet, " 'I am at rest with you—I have come home.' "[16]

To the end of her life Dorothy L. Sayers continued to enjoy the London Detection Club, a group whose mock-ceremonies she had composed, whose leader she was until her death. She loved to dress up (like Harriet Vane on her wedding day) in gold lame with great dangling earrings, and talk with wit and relish of plots and "jiggery-pokery" and the craft of fiction. Though a shy woman, she was exuberant and articulate with friends, and was a dynamic public figure, majestic and dignified and delightful in her role.

The form of the detective novel had given shape to her life at a time when she desperately needed it. She could set a problem and solve it in a neat intellectual manner, a comfort indeed to a bright woman faced with complex, intractable, and unsolvable problems in her real life. Certainly life itself seldom operated so simply. To the end of her life, she worked at and planned to complete the study of Wilkie Collins, her favorite detective writer. Sayers, as one of the first scholars to turn her attention to this neglected popular form, gave the detective story shape and respectability. Perhaps she had originally turned to crime writing for money, but she discovered in it fun, fame, and a sense of vocation. A long and happy relationship with her publisher—Gollancz—and an enthusiastic audience brought her material comfort and artistic authority. By doing the work which lay at hand and doing it with all her heart, she found that no work need be cheap or degrading. The right person can ennoble it.

The angry haunted period of Sayers' life was over. She had found a path through the Valley of Humiliation and the Valley of the Shadow and was joyfully back on the King's Highway. She was now ready to turn to her more direct testimonies of the thrilling love of God and to a new community of believers—not the church, but the theatre.

Chronology of the Detective Stories

1923	*Whose Body?*
1926	*Clouds of Witness*
1927	*Unnatural Death*
1928	*The Unpleasantness at the Bellona Club*
	Lord Peter Views the Body (short stories)
	Great Stories of Detection, Mystery, and Horror, First Series (the first *Omnibus of Crime*, selections by other authors, introduction by Sayers)
1930	*The Documents in the Case* (with Robert Eustace [Eustace Robert Barton])
	Strong Poison
	series of essays on detection in periodicals
1931	*The Five Red Herrings*
	The Omnibus of Crime, Second Series
1932	*Have His Carcase*
1933	*Murder Must Advertise*
	Hangman's Holiday (short stories)
1934	*The Nine Tailors*
	The Omnibus of Crime, Third Series
1935	*Gaudy Night*
1936	"Papers Relating to the Family of Wimsey" (booklet)
1937	*Busman's Honeymoon* (play in collaboration with Muriel St. Clare Byrne)
	Busman's Honeymoon (novel)
1939	*In the Teeth of the Evidence and Other Stories* (short stories)

V. *On the King's Highway*

The gradual abandonment of Lord Peter was inevitable. He had served his purpose by the mid-thirties—the support of his creator and her family, the establishment of her reputation as an author.

Although Benson's Advertising Agency had provided Dorothy Sayers with a practical education essential for the sheltered girl from the rectory in the fen country, she had little respect for the work she found herself called upon to perform. As she demonstrated in *Murder Must Advertise*, a novel she said she "hated," the necessary catering to the lowest common denominator of public taste was degrading. The puffery of products regardless of their real value she came to see as basically dishonest. Though the people in the industry were often witty and entertaining, they were just as often dissolute and egotistical. The unworthy use of talents, the failure to discover or to develop in one's true vocation, eventually, according to her view, ended in bitterness and brutality. (This warping process she describes vividly in a Lord Peter short story which pictures an artist-turned-killer.) Sayers found herself very successful in slogan-writing and in the mounting of advertising campaigns. She was aware that the constant demands of the profession had sharpened her writing skills and had made her sensitive to the demands of an audience. But as soon as she had achieved financial security through her other writing, she resigned her job with Benson's.

Lord Peter himself had gradually grown older, and, like Dorothy Sayers, had also grown more serious. The moral verities grew for him less distinguishable, and he grew less certain he wanted to be the unraveler of mystery or the means for setting legal machinery in motion. The murderer he unmasked on his honeymoon left him in tears.

On another occasion his discovery that a brilliant young artist suddenly and fatally attacked a thoroughly despicable roue demanded a report to the police, but not conclusive proof. Both he and the police were ready to dismiss the case. For once, Lord Peter was content to let a dead man be blamed for the crime of a living one. Humanity rather than abstract justice was thereby served. He had grown weary of simplistic, often cruel human justice, based on people's known actions without sufficient concern for their justifications. This increasing distrust of the black-white value system of the world of detective fiction appears to be a natural outgrowth of Sayers' own dabbling in disgrace and her sympathetic imagination. Her care for her illicit child, her divorced husband, the contrast between her public image and private reality helped her to develop a compassion for the outcast—even, in select cases, for the criminal. In her maturing, she discovered the motives for evil action and the varieties of evil to be more complex than physical violence alone would suggest. The psychology of evil and the theology and experience of God's forgiveness led Dorothy L. Sayers increasingly into an exploration of the more complex world of religious drama.

Lord Peter helped in the transition. *Gaudy Night* had left the British public titillated with expectation of further revelations regarding the romance with Harriet Vane. The wedding clearly deserved a novel to demonstrate the proper practice of marriage between civilized, intelligent, sensitive people. It also promised to be the natural conclusion to the series.

With the encouragement of her old school friend, the Elizabethan scholar Muriel St. Clare Byrne, Dorothy Sayers undertook to write a stage version of the Wimsey honeymoon. The two friends experimented with dialogue and dramaturgy, gradually developing the script for a play they called *Busman's Honeymoon.* Janet Hitchman, in her biography of Dorothy Sayers, describes the shuttling back and forth of manuscripts, with Sayers providing the ideas and Byrne editing them for the stage.[1] Using the comedy-of-manners form that Sayers had polished in the Wimsey novels, the two friends brought the same brittle repartee and affected manners to the stage. The play conformed nicely to the taste of the early twentieth-century English theatergoing public; the witty, artificial dialogue had proven popular from Oscar Wilde to Noel Coward, continuing an older line of Restoration and eighteenth-century comedy. She uses the newly wedded couple's arrival at their recently purchased run-down country home, Talboys, where the disarray of impedimenta proved a rude shock to poor Bunter. The mystery of the absentee landlord is finally expanded to a larger mystery—how was he murdered, by whom, and why? And the contrast between the manners of London sophisticates and county folk (especially between Bunter and the other hired help) proves the source for delightful comedy. *Busman's Honeymoon* ran for nine months in London, with a "mix" of judgments by critics.[2] Later, Sayers completed and published a narrative version as well; but the novel, like the play, demonstrates more interest in love than in murder, a clear indication of her change of heart signaled already in the murderless *Gaudy Night*.

Though a few short stories dribbled out in later years, telling of the birth and rearing of the Wimsey children, Dorothy Sayers was content that she had completed the murderous phase of her life. She had collected world-famous mysteries in three volumes with impressive introductions that testify to her understanding of the form; she had collaborated with other members of the London Detection Club to write some serials; she had written a host of novels in addition to stories that had critics calling her the best detective writer since Sir Arthur Conan Doyle. By now an acknowledged master of the form, she needed a new challenge and a more serious use of her art. This she discovered in the theater and in religious drama. Advertising had taught her a great deal about public taste; novels had developed her skill in characterization, plotting, and development of theme. Now God called her to his service in the theater.

Her first great opportunity for exploring this new arena came in 1936, when the Friends of Canterbury approached her with a proposal to write a play for the 1937 Canterbury Festival. The invitation came as the fulfillment of a growing inclination to develop her own chancel drama; she had already considered drama and its relationship to the worship of God over a number of years, starting with her adolescent work *The Mocking of Christ.* Her relationship with organized religion was respectful but not blind—witness her laughter at the parishioners in *The Nine Tailors* and her lack of enthusiasm for church socials. Hitchman reports that the members of her own home parish were deeply disturbed that she elected simplicity over display in the burial of her parents, not even purchasing gravestones to mark their burial. She was willing to argue theology with a bishop as freely and vivaciously as with a schoolmate. She responded deeply to the order of the service, the creeds and the traditions of the institutional church, but had her reservations about the day-to-day activities and pronouncements of churchmen. Her own varied life experience, and her inclination to fraternize with and love publicans and sinners would have made her anathema to many churchgoing people. She habitually spoke openly and colorfully of a full range of human experience, and she delighted in indulging her medieval taste for the bawdy. She was not given to keeping silent—in church or elsewhere. And eventually she came to outrage a substantial body of colorless, unthinking Christians who subscribed blindly to what she called the "Seven Deadly Virtues." She thought (and announced that she thought) that much of the Christian community had lost its savor and her goal was to supply the salt.

In later years, she was to come back into a closer communion with the established church—less at Witham than at St. Thomas, Regent Street and its sister parish, St. Anne's in Soho, where she sought along with some others to restore some zest to Christian living and thinking. She was a vicar's warden there and an active participant in intellectual activities, along with such distinguished citizens as Sir Harold Nicholson and Sir Herbert Read.[3]

Of course, she had always loved the faith itself. Life had taught her the validity of many of the creeds and rituals, and she increasingly felt the need to testify to their relevance to contemporary life. In the drama she saw the opportunity to show others the Way.

As a scholar who had never abandoned her studies, she brought to the modern scene a broad perspective. She saw the dreariness of contemporary English Christianity against a background of fierce battles for the creeds of the church. For the intellectually alert Christian, every word of the Nicene Creed was full of semantic and theological riches. While the artistic and intellectual community wandered vaguely in search of faddish new values, lamenting faintly the ache of modernism, Sayers understood the clear and present hope for humanity in the proper use of the past. Rejecting the fragmented vision of the aesthetes or the liberal humanism of the intellectuals, she was a medievalist who saw little value in originality for its own sake. She sought truth where generations of fellow humans had discovered it—in the life and teachings of Christ. Rather than abandoning the institutional, dehumanized, and demythologized Jesus of the established church, she ripped off the veil of custom to discover the incredible profundity of Christ, man and God. She showed us how to become salty Christians once again.

This hard-won conservatism of Dorothy Sayers was no simplistic, ritualistic Sunday school recitation. She, like Paul, insisted that the Christian must abandon pap for "strong meat." Her words have vigor because her ideas are built on solid theological foundations and on broad individual experience. She had discovered the truth of Scripture for herself existentially and was hungry to share her lively discoveries with others.

It was fitting that this perennial scholar should consider the historical roots of drama as well as the theology. The movement from novel to drama was to be a fundamental reconsideration of form as well as function. While her use of the novel was discursive, realistic, witty, mannered, and modern, she was to use the drama as a more compact, universal, stylized form. The chatter of the characters in her novels was to be replaced by the tightly organized dialogue in her plays. The omniscient author had to become the more obtrusive onstage narrator; the prose was to be replaced by poetry. Her use of character, dialogue, setting, plot, theme, and structure changes with her change in form. In considering this significant selection of a different genre, one capable of greater heights and therefore offering greater challenges, she also considered its different demands on author and audience. And she considered the history of the drama as a key to its meaning as a form.

She knew that the medieval "mystery" cycle was derived from the old French word *mystere*, which meant "scripture." This antique folk drama which entertained European and English citizens of the Middle

Ages was to become the basis of modern theater. In cities such as York and Chester, the guilds had sponsored these religious entertainments, which had developed out of the liturgy of the church, but which had quickly outgrown the sanctuary and broken free of the clergy. Those plays whose manuscripts are still extant show these medieval plays to be short, often singsong and clumsy, but nonetheless charming and lively. An early example is the "Quem Quaeritis" trope, a simple question-answer dialogue between Mary and the angel on Easter.

In addition to such plays based on Scripture, there were also miracles (plays based on saints' lives), and moralities (plays in which abstractions, such as the Seven Deadly Sins, might be personified and marched onto the stage for the audience's edification). Interludes, or entertainments between the acts of a play, might have included jugglers, dancers, and bawdy singers. Even in the Scriptural dramas, the now-forgotten authors felt free to include slapstick, horseplay, and crude jokes. Their brutality was often grotesque, their symbolism startlingly literal.

If we consider the nature of Chaucer's pilgrims on their journey to Canterbury, we have some notion of the fantastic mixture of religious responses among medieval men and women. Dorothy L. Sayers included some of these in her first Canterbury play, *The Zeal of Thy House*, in which she portrayed the pilgrims as modern tourists. "One in ten may be sincere," the sacristan complains. "The rest are idle men and gadding women, making pilgrimage an excuse for a holiday trip." He laments that they compound "old sins by committing new ones." They do not come to worship, but all they come for is "to drink and gossip in alehouses, tell each other dirty stories, pick up loose companions, waste their own time and other people's, and gabble through a few perfunctory prayers at top speed, so as to have more time for sightseeing."[4] They sound, in brief, much like modern tourists at Canterbury Cathedral.

But even if medieval Christians were no better than we, their festivals do seem to have been more fun than ours, more like the Oberammergau plays or the Spanish saints festivals. Corpus Christi, for example, was often given over to the medieval dramatic productions. The old scripts were dusted off and adjusted to the new year, assigned to various guilds according to interests and equipment (bakers or vintners might handle the Last Supper, carpenters or ironmongers the crucifixion). The wagons (or "pageants") were prepared, fitted out with simple scenery. The costumes were refurbished, angel wings refeathered and crowns polished. The parts might have been taken in some cases by professionals, but often amateurs learned their parts and enjoyed their brief fling as actors. (Herod was a particular favorite villain role, usually played in ranting tones with an Italian accent.)

In the English tradition, each "pageant" or wagon contained one play in the cycle; it would be repeated in various parts of the town and would be followed by other wagons, unveiling their segments of the great story stretching from Creation to the Apocalypse. Especial favorites were Noah, Arbraham and Isaac, Moses and Pharaoh, and the Passion of Christ.

Although commercialization and secularization gradually and repeatedly (after new beginnings) converted the theater into an enemy of the church, the ecclesiastical basis for drama has never been entirely erased. Efforts to reconcile the warring parties have been frequent and sometimes successful in the twentieth century. The increasing popularity of chancel drama has signaled a temporary reconciliation at last.

Dorothy Sayers understood the natural relationships between these old kinsmen-enemies; the very experience of Easter struck her as "the greatest drama ever staged." Certainly the role of God in human history has the immediacy and excitement of drama. The dialogue between humans and God is mirrored in the dialogue of the drama. And the dynamic pattern of revelation through experience is the very soul of dramatic form. It is no accident that in both ancient Greece and medieval Christendom, the theater grew out of worship. In her constant search for the essential nature of human life and thought, Dorothy Sayers was destined to discover the value of the theater for her own expression: she admired the characters acting within the total framework as free agents, just as actual people work freely in God's world. She could, in the drama, more freely mingle natural and supernatural elements; and she could draw on some of her old talent for poetic expression. She could include a narrator to provide supernatural commentary, serving as chorus. The realism demanded by the world of the detective story could be replaced by the poetry and grandeur of the theater.

At last she could abandon Lord Peter's constant concern for the right tie and the best wine and move on to the great moral and theological questions that torment the modern soul. Even Lord Peter had in his later days showed increasing sensitivity to moral and religious issues, but it was not in keeping with his eighteenth-century gentility to become a Christian convert. He could show respect for high-church views and admire ecclesiastical architecture, even participate in the parish worship, but Dorothy L. Sayers needed a new means to present the case for Christianity. She found it in the drama.

Her friend Charles Williams had written *Thomas Cranmer of Canterbury* for the 1936 Canterbury Festival, causing Sayers to hesitate at the invitation. She did not see herself as his and Eliot's successor: "I don't want to mug up the history of kings and archbishops."[5] Sayers was convinced to undertake the work only when she heard that the 1937 Festival was to be a Service of Arts and Crafts. To this she could enthusiastically respond; in her choice of subject (the building of the new choir), in her medium (the mystery plays used by the medieval guilds), and in her method (pitching in like the old craftsmen to feather angels and polish crowns).

When asked to write the Canterbury play, Sayers could hardly ignore the brilliant precedent set by T. S. Eliot with *Murder in the Cathedral*. Certain of his practices appealed to her so much that she incorporated them into her own play: for example, his use of the history of the building itself and of the clergy as characters. While he dealt with the murder of Thomas à Becket, she skipped over the fire which followed the murder (those very elements that would have provided the mystery for Lord Peter to unravel) and concentrated on the rebuilding. Her hero is the secular architect chosen for the reconstruction, but William is surrounded by a cast much like Eliot's: citizens of the parish, ecclesiastics, and choir members. Like Eliot, Sayers contrasts the poetry of the service itself and the more philosophic segments of the play with the prose of the common folk. The contemporary accents break colorfully through the antique tale and reinforce the enduring patterns of human conduct. Sayers' background in church music inclined her to include more liturgical music than Eliot did; her love of church architecture (already apparent in the Wimsey novels) led her to use the symbolism of the building itself in a thoroughly satisfying and appropriately medieval manner. For example, outlining the church of his dream, William describes it in these words:

> Arch shouldering arch, shaft, vault and keystone, window and arcading higher, and wider and lighter, lifting roof, tower, spire, into the vault of heaven—columns slender as lily-stalks—walls only a framework for the traceries—living fountains of stone.[6]

The humble workman at his side interrupts to point the symbol that emerges: "That's so, Master, that's so. That's the way to build. Each stone carrying his neighbour's burden, as you might say." Then William places the image back into the larger structure of God's world with its glory and its majesty: "A triumph of balance."[7] The importance of this symbolism was to haunt Sayers until she finally developed the whole set of ideas more fully in her translation and explication of Dante.

The Zeal of Thy House describes the legend of William, a consummate craftsman, an imaginative architect, and an unregenerate sinner. The separation of craft and craftsman, the public work and the private man, would naturally appeal to Dorothy L. Sayers as she faced her sense of vocation and her haunting fear of the world's unkind judgment on her unpublicized private life. Some of William's trickery appears to have a valid rationale—the glory of the completed masterpiece. If he must resort to deception and lies, in dealing with the secular and clerical grafters who handle the finances and the supplies, he accepts the principle that the end justifies the means and acts with a comparatively clear conscience. But his undisguised lust, which he openly indulges with a widow in the parish, and his unbridled pride in his creation drive him deeper and deeper into sin. In a climactic scene, he apparently challenges God in his creativity and his freedom:

> We are the master-craftsmen, God and I—
> We understand one another.

After describing in beautifully poetic terms the days of the creation, he confronts God with these words:

> And lastly, since all Heaven was not enough
> To share that triumph, He made His masterpiece,
> Man, that like God can call beauty from dust,
> Order from chaos, and create new worlds

To praise their maker. Oh, but in making man
God over-reached Himself and gave away
His Godhead. He must now depend on man
For what man's brain, creative and divine
Can give Him. Man stands equal with Him now,
Partner and rival.[8]

Thus, as the horrified listeners gasp, William forces God to show him that, though unique, he is not indispensable. Disaster follows immediately on the hubris. Watching him, the monks fail to test the rope on which he will swing toward heaven; the rope breaks, the machinery falls, and William is painfully and permanently crippled. This literal and figurative fall by no means completes the Christian drama, for crippling of the body leads to William's discovery of God's love as well as God's power. And through divine love, he finds the truth of human love. Like the Greeks, Sayers is convinced that we learn through suffering. And William's lessons prove rich ones. By the end of the play, William has found that he is not and should not seek to be self-sufficient. He needs other hands to help with his work and to complete it; and he needs the enduring power of God to preserve that which he has partially accomplished. The worship before the shrine of his own artistry is transformed into the worship of God. He exchanges his egocentric humanism for Christian humility.

The play, though overly contrived and somewhat stiff, is nonetheless a lucid, poetic, Christian statement of considerable power. It combines wit, poetry, romance, bawdy songs, angelic choirs, history, and imagination in an impressive and mature statement. Other books were to be more forthright: *Are Women Human?* expresses more fully Sayers' view on women; *The Mind of the Maker* explores her aesthetic theories in greater detail. But *The Zeal of Thy House* is the sharpest, most succinct dramatic statement of the maturing philosophy of Dorothy L. Sayers. Its greatest flaw is its excessive neatness and polish. It is too tidy to be real.

Two years later she sought to repeat her success, but could not bring the same vitality to the medieval Faust legend. Though *The Devil to Pay* also focuses on Sayers' concern with evil, it is less effective than her later studies of the same subject. As an attack on that modern liberalism which seeks to trivialize evil and deny the existence of the devil, it is an interesting play. It certainly points to her rejection of the Romantic notion of basic human goodness. But her later presentations of Judas and of Christ are a better demonstration of the same ideas—the choices a man must make in his life, the price he must pay for those choices, and the reality of evil. Even if *The Devil to Pay* is not her strongest portrayal of the forces of evil, it is nonetheless an interesting play in its reworking of the Faust legend for contemporary audiences. And it proved a valuable preparation for more demanding work that was to follow.

In this play, Faustus is a thinly disguised modern humanist, convinced of his own ability to redeem evil in the world and of our basic human perfectability. This is altogether in keeping with the work of Goethe, but differs impressively in the author's point of view and the consequent shape of the play. Faustus is arrogant enough to believe he can eradicate evil through material well-being, bringing the kingdom of God to earth. But people immediately create new evils from Faustus's generous showers of gold: the strong rob the weak and leave them in more pitiful condition than before his beneficence. Disappointed by the bleakly Darwinian struggle that results from his philanthropy, Faustus turns to human love, assuming that the solution lies in individual relationships, but again his vague idealism destroys the hope for human happiness. Rejecting the mundane human satisfaction he could know with a real woman, he elects the dream of Helen, an abstract symbol of Venus.

Sayers analyzed Goethe's Faust and Marlowe's Faustus thoroughly before she drafted this work. Goethe's Romantic notion of salvation-in-striving struck her as unrealistic and anti-Christian. Our own efforts can by no means effect our salvation or that of any other human being. We are saved solely by the grace of God. Marlowe's tragic hero also echoed the predominant dream of his age, the Renaissance love of knowledge and the dream of unlimited capacity for development. For the modern, this liberal faith is a flirtation with damnation; for it elevates humanity and temporal happiness while denying the value of suffering and of redemption. Satan is better interpreted by Dante: the epitome of hate, the negative aspect of God, the shadow that comes from the presence of light. It is consequently this vision that Sayers uses in her play—an interesting foreshadowing of her later attraction to Dante.

Her setting is appropriately medieval with heavenly mansions on one side of the stage and the mouth of hell on the other. (In some medieval plays, the townspeople hauled the skeleton of a whale's head to the theater for the jaws of hell.) The language is appropriately antique so as to match this tale of witchcraft and supernatural struggle; the play is a modern morality play where good angels and bad fight over the soul of Everyman. The poetry occasionally echoes Marlowe, occasionally Goethe, and occasionally George Bernard Shaw. No mixture seems too outrageous for this impressively eclectic playwright to employ.

The Devil to Pay is a parallel study to *The Zeal of Thy House*, presenting the spiritual issues raised there from another perspective. These brilliant and talented dreamers (William and Faustus) share egotism, faith in humanity, and in themselves. Each of them must suffer failure to achieve recognition and final spiritual fulfillment. Again, Sayers is blending medieval and classical form in an effort to discover the best mode for Christian drama. She is also portraying her own journey through pain into salvation.

Another experiment in chancel drama, using still another mode, proved even less successful than *The Devil to Pay.* Although friends note that Sayers considered *The Just Vengeance* her best drama (and *Zeal* her worst), we must realize that most writers are poor judges of their own work. From her earliest writing efforts, Dorothy Sayers had been in love with poetry. She had a good ear for the beauty of other authors' poetry and a talent for music that gave the play a degree of power and majesty.

As she notes in the introduction, the play was drawn from two passages she had read and meditated upon, one from *The Divine Comedy* and the other from Thomas à Kempis. The central problem is the "just avenging" or the "just vengeance" in the crucifixion. Those of us who worried over issues with Lord Peter can trace the theme all through her work. As she indicates, "In form, the drama is a miracle-play of Man's insufficiency and God's redemptive act, set against a background of contemporary crisis." The play is set in Lichfield, where George Fox, founder of the Quakers, cried out his ominous vision of blood on the city. "The whole action," Sayers notes, "takes place in the moment of the death of an Airman shot down during the late war."[9] His active involvement with vengeance (against the Nazis) forms a strong contrast with Fox's passive resistance, allowing each to argue his position. Then, asked to affirm his real beliefs, the Airman pronounces his vague humanism in effective counterpoint with the choir's chanting of the Creed:

> I believe in man, and in the hope of the future,
> The steady growth of knowledge and power over things,
> The equality of all labouring for the community,
> And a just world where everyone will be happy.[10]

Since such flabby humanism can hardly redeem him at this extreme moment of his life, he is shown a vision of the fall, of the first vengeance (Cain and Abel), and of the redemption through Christ. "There," notes Sayers, "being shown in an image the meaning of the Atonement, he accepts the Cross, and passes, in that act of choice, from the image to the reality.[11]

The Just Vengeance, clearly a meditation on the role of the Christian community in war and on the role of Christ in the redemption of the sinner, was written in 1946, for Lichfield Cathedral's 750th anniversary. As in other chancel plays, she combines the setting of the cathedral, the role of the choir as chorus, the litanies and music of the church, along with bits of local history and universal Christian faith. As always in this form, she concentrates her thoughts on the miracle and meaning of the incarnation.

A more powerful example of her zeal for doctrine and her love of the creeds may be found in her final chancel drama, *The Emperor Constantine*, which appeared in 1951, for the Colchester Festival. The play, a magnificent, though flawed *tour de force*, bears witness to the enormous zeal Dorothy L. Sayers brought to even modest requests. Works celebrating an occasion, especially chancel dramas, are generally expected to be pompous and forgettable. Instead of grinding out the obligatory Scriptural paraphrase, she snatched the thread of tradition that Old King Cole (Coel), his pipe, and his fiddlers three belonged to the city of Colchester. Since Coel was purported to be the father of Constance and the grandfather of Constantine, Sayers used him and his prophecies to frame a play about the career of Emperor Constantine and the drafting of the Nicene Creed.

Demonstrating her rich knowledge of history and her delight in reconstructing historical settings, *The Emperor Constantine* tells the convoluted tale of Constantine, the enigmatic emperor who wrenched the Roman Empire back into unity and imperiously converted it to Christianity. He was hardly a classic Christian saint: he divorced one wife, killed another, murdered his firstborn son, exiled and executed both colleagues and relatives. His virtues were a strong mind, a seeking spirit, and devotion to his mother. He was a complex man, a part of a complex period, confronting complex theological and political questions. He could hardly be expected to lend himself to a simple drama.

Therefore, Sayers abandoned her usual medievalism and sought a form closer to Shakespeare's chronicle plays. She covers the years from Constantine's youth till his death; she selects characters to present confliciting views; she focuses on those points in his life most crucial to the understanding of his character and his actions. Battles are offstage, intrigues are commonplace, and corpses are plentiful. To explain the rationale for this brilliant and basically decent man's violence toward his son and his wife, Sayers adopted the myth of Phaedra, the woman who fell in love with her stepson and framed him through a perjured attack on his virtue. The father, in this case Constantine, believes the wife and kills the son without even considering the possibility of her connivance.

The central scene in the story, however, deals not with Constantine's convoluted family problems, but with the Council of Nicaea—that great council called to decide between the rival claims of Athanasius and Arius. Sayers handles the controversy well, pointing to the subtle linguistic and philosophic differences in wording, dramatizing the need for absolute clarity in order to quash the heresy of unitarianism and to assert the divinity of Christ.

A later scene, which serves as the turning point for Constantine himself, is the murder of his son, followed by the recognition of his wife's deceit. In a blinding flash, he realizes that he himself is an evil man, so drenched in sin he cannot extricate himself from it without a redeemer. The sorrowful but necessary execution of his wife and the politically expedient cleaning up of the conspiracy, which had used her, are the hideous consequences of sin. Meditating on his own innocent son, slain for the sin of others, he experiences insight into the pain and love of God. The action reinforces, parallels, and contrasts with the crucifixion, making flesh out of a doctrine he had previously seen as reasonable rather than true. Driven to his knees by his conviction of his own sin, Constantine finally acknowledges his own need of God's grace, and is eventually baptized a Christian.

The play is far too complex for the modern theatergoer to follow with ease or understanding. It is too full of history, theology, subtle philosophic points, classical allusions, linguistic quibbling—though every part is handled with style and zest. It is the impressive failure of a scholar who enjoys using her mind and who demands the same vitality of other Christians. As theater, the play scarcely works. It is simply too stuffed to be clear. It suffers from too much matter—or what she later termed too much "Idea." (In *The Mind of the Maker* she calls such unbalanced failures "scalene trinities.")

Some years before Dorothy Sayers had come upon the challenge presented by the Colchester Festival, she had confronted her greatest dramatic challenge, the opportunity to write a cycle of plays for the radio. *The Man Born to Be King* was to prove her greatest dramatic triumph and to win her her largest popular audience.

The British Broadcasting Company had been toying with the idea of producing a series of radio dramas on the life of Christ. Her earlier nativity play, *He That Should Come*, had already proved a modest success with radio audiences, as had some of her mystery stories, and she was becoming something of a radio celebrity. She had given a number of talks on various subjects for BBC, and her Lord Peter stories were being dramatized to the delight of old fans and new ones. The moment seemed right to ask her to draft the plays. Thus, in March 1940, Reverend J. W. Welch, the Director of Religious Broadcasting for BBC, wrote Sayers suggesting that she do the series. Her eager acceptance of the offer was qualified by her insistence that she be allowed to present Christ as a character (at the time, an illegal action in stage presentations in Great Britain), and that she be allowed to use modern idiom (an outrageous sacrilege in the eyes of those who venerated the King James Version as if it were the original Holy Writ).

She decided quickly on the form, a kind of modernized mystery cycle, tied together through the use of a narrator, repetition of characters, continuing theme, and consistent style. She visualized the scenes vividly, presenting them for the listening audience in a remarkable sensitive manner: aware of the need for sound effects, varied rhythms and tones of speech, interruptions for surprise, explanations of difficult points, and a realistic sense of comedy. Her development of each of the characters is clearly outlined in her introductory notes, versions of which she made available to the play's producer.

Her choice of unifying themes conforms to her long-standing interests. Her faith in the centrality of the incarnation led her to think deeply about the person of Christ as the express image of God. Her awareness of God's power led her to speculate on the challenge that the incarnation necessarily presented to all other forms of earthly and spiritual power. As she noted, there is a "great dispute going on about how the world should be governed, and to what end."[12] The claims of Christ are obvious in such a war for control over human destiny.

As in a number of her other plays, she considered the Christian use of adversity. Her own experience of sin and suffering brought depth and texture to her interpretation. Christ, as the hero, goes majestically through suffering to reconciliation with God. Judas, by contrast, takes the Faustian path of social redemption, finally understands his own betrayal, seeks to make restitution in his own terms, and finds that human beings alone cannot erase their evil. Sayers explores the character of Peter as the backslider, who contrasts dramatically with Judas the apostate. While Peter can acknowledge the full horror of his sin and throw himself on the mercy of God, Judas has chosen to deny the power of the Holy Spirit and therefore has elected his own damnation.

The characters are fully developed, provided with histories and psychology and relationships and accents and tastes that make them thoroughly human. She simplified the enormous body of followers and adversaries by blending them into types and carrying some of them through all of the stories. She expanded a few of the characters into complex studies with interesting motives based on fully developed psychological and religious histories. She kept the old English tradition of the three kings and used them to bracket her plays—at the nativity and again at the crucifixion.

Her stage directions demonstrate her enthusiasm for the details of production. Apparently she enjoyed rehearsals and insisted—much to the distress of numerous officials at BBC—on selecting certain talents she thought most compatible with her ideas. In her chancel plays, she was known to have lent a hand with props and costumes, enjoying the camaraderie of the theater troupe. Benjamin Britten composed music for the work, and Val Gielgud agreed to direct it. As the time for the presentation approached, it promised to be an exciting radio event.

Unfortunately, on the eve of the first broadcast, the newspapers headlined her use of contemporary speech, leading to a premature flurry of outrage among a number of church groups, notably the Lord's Day Observance Society and the Protestant Truth Society.[13] The presentation of Christ speaking his own words appalled the entrenched Protestant iconoclasts, who prophesied that this would be the beginning of a deluge of Scriptural parodies.

In spite of the negative predictions, the plays themselves tended to carry the day. Her originality (presenting, for example, in her first play, an understandable Herod deliberately planning to slaughter the innocents), her realism, her humor, her understanding of universal humanity made the plays a triumph. They testify to her very real belief in the truth of Scripture, not just as historical fact, but as universal insight. While her age seemed content to reduce Jesus to a tinsel decoration for the Christmas tree or a stiff image in the stained glass window, she reminded them that he was human and divine. They had, she noted, committed the horrendous sin of making him dull—one thing which Christ never was. As she had noted at the beginning of her career, the Easter story itself was the greatest drama ever staged, and the incarnation was the most exciting event in human history. At long last, she marshaled her considerable talent to express her delight and amazement at this magnificent drama of God entering human history.

She asked that the series not be repeated so often as to become a seasonal ritual. And she requested that it not be televised. Later, after her death, when plans were going forward for a TV series on Jesus of Nazareth, the writers drew heavily from her plays, though her name did not appear in the credits. She would have resented, not the use of her work, for she frequently used others' the same way, but the watering down of her ideas. For her, the miracles were rich with meaning, not problems to be explained away. She was not embarrassed by Christ's divinity. Her rejection of television was primarily because of the commercial interruptions that she thought improper in good art or theology.

She did draw heavily on Hebrew tradition in the plays, showing her respect for Jesus' Jewish heritage. If she had been anti-Semitic earlier, and concerned about the influx of Jewish immigrants into Britain, she does not show it here. Her plays have none of the stereotyped villain in Herod or Caiaphas in medieval mysteries or rock musicals. Her Jews are fully realized humans. Perhaps the study of Matthew and John changed her heart and enlarged her vision.

In *The Man Born to Be King*, as in all of her works, Dorothy L. Sayers demonstrated her control of words, her love of form, her wide knowledge of literature, history, and theology, her unpretentious simplicity and directness in presentation, and her existential commitment to her faith. The cycle, which was more successful on radio and in book form than she had dared hope, was the culminating effort of her middle years. It combined her medieval tastes and knowledge, her theology, her skill in technique, and her own discoveries about human life and divine grace in one beautiful series.

As form, it proved a triumph for her, a demonstration that drama is the almost perfect form for presentation of theology. Christ had himself stepped onto the stage of this world, perceived by others and known to them through his words and actions, and by the words and actions of others who touched his life. He developed from infancy to manhood, matured into an understanding of his ministry and his sacrifice. His life followed a dynamic pattern, with rising action, suspense, intrigue, surprise, and contrast. That the climax was a majestic piece of poetic irony, demanding recognition on the part of the disciples and the modern audience alike, is especially suitable to the drama. Like the religious service, its closest relative, carefully wrought chancel drama makes demands on its audience/participants, presenting a challenge and providing a direction. It need not be the whimsical imagining of a talented artist or the careful construction of an able artisan, but can in fact be an act of worship.

Sayers' exploration of this field of art proved enormously rewarding to her: she found here an ever-expanding audience for her literary work, her theology, and her philosophy; she found she could grow in her understanding of her faith; and she found the form aesthetically satisfying. In a sense, she also found community. For most of her life, she had sought to be part of such a group. It should have been in the church, but she so often found herself ill at ease in the organized church, so disappointed in its leaders and members, so upset that it was forgetting its mission, that she could not relax with the church.

For most people, the most basic community is the family; but since the death of her parents, Dorothy Sayers had little hope in family. Her husband drank himself into a stupor each evening at the local pub, and she sought a neighbor to help bring him home. Fleming disliked seeing her at work, so she stole her working time from the hours he was out of the house. They could find some common pleasure in their animals—laughing at the bawdy language of the parrot or the antics of the many cats—but they seem to have made a truce rather than a home. The son was off at school, visiting only on vacations, not really a significant part of their lives.

Her Oxford cronies—especially Helen Simpson and Muriel St. Clare Byrne—and some other writers were good friends, but not regular companions she could rely on from day to day. The Inklings, on the other hand, that convivial group of Oxford Christians who clustered around C. S. Lewis, had their evenings together on a regular basis. Dorothy Sayers sought out local folk she met on late evening walks to come and share a glass of sherry with her—sometimes huddled snugly in the boiler room of her Witham cottage for warmth.

She knew that people still judged her for the wrong things—for a wrinkled skirt or baggy slacks—rather than for her real values. At a play rehearsal, she could crawl around among the sets, work with the costumes, shout suggestions to the actors in a happy freedom. When audiences commented on her tennis shoes, she sent for her academic robes and wandered around the cathedral with her daily wear hidden from view. She enjoyed the jolly mood and the sense of shared goals she found in the theater. As she told a group of young people one night in bomb-plagued London, she found in the theater that spirit of mutual support and affection she had missed in the church—"a happy mutuality of creation, like Charles Williams' vision of the City."[14]

She did consider and write other plays. One short run in London was *Love All* in 1940 (earlier titled *Cat's Cradle*), a sophisticated comedy about a liberated woman who finds herself a success in the theater after being badly treated by her wayward husband. She also considered writing a war play, based on an episode from Froissart, but she never got it written.[15]

Several of her plays, notably the Lichfield drama, echo the troubled days in which they were written. With the outbreak of war in Britain, she was to use her new opportunities to preach Christian wisdom to confused and frightened fellow Britons. Her plays reflect the concerns of a threatened people, sobered by the face-to-face confrontation with death or enslavement. She called upon the English to consider the meaning of life and to look beyond the battle for survival to perceive the battle for meaning. Such books as *Creed or Chaos?* defend her beloved creeds and demonstrate their relevance to a people needing a foundation on which to rebuild. She mocks with gentle irony the shallow piety of the British and demands a vigorous new faith, a sense of vocation, a thrill at the reality of the incarnation. Her plays had opened the door for serious and widespread consideration of her ideas. Increasingly, she was invited to speak of aesthetics, modernism, patriotism, sin, salvation, and feminism. In the middle of the journey of her life, she found herself famous.

Chronology of the Drama

1918	*The Mocking of Christ*
1937	*Busman's Honeymoon*
	The Zeal of Thy House
1939	*He That Should Come*
	The Devil to Pay
1940	*Love All* (at first called *Cat's Cradle*)
1943	*The Man Born to Be King*
1946	*The Just Vengeance*
1951	*The Emperor Constantine*

VI. *The View from the Delectable Mountains*

Dorothy L. Sayers was becoming a public person at about the same time that England was being drawn into war. This impressive woman with her no-nonsense gray suit (complete with innumerable pockets, because she refused to carry a purse), her hand-knitted woolen stockings (which, she announced with pride, were made by her own hands), and her porkpie hat (like a clergyman of the Middle Ages) could march to the front of an audience with authority. Her eyes twinkling behind thick, rimless glasses, her voice deep and strong and full of feeling, she electrified her audiences. In response to a comment that she did not look very attractive in trousers, she responded that for the moment she did not seek to attract anyone but only to be comfortable. She had decided that she had no one to please by her clothing but herself. She bought good clothes, but of nondescript appearance. Rarely did she care what she wore. There was no doubt who Dorothy L. Sayers was or where she stood. She was never more at ease with herself. Her speeches were organized, logical, clear, and funny. More than one person who heard her during those dark days said that her speech changed their lives.

James Brabazon, her official biographer, first saw her during the Blitz when she spoke to a room full of young people about the theater. Forty years later, he could still recall much of her humor, her dramatic emphasis, and the substance of her talk. Another biographer-friend, who met her somewhat later, recalls another of her speeches. Dr. Barbara Reynolds had invited her to speak on Dante to a group of Italian scholars at Cambridge. Again, the impressive presence, the great voice, the poise, the careful phrasing, and the delightful wit combined with a powerful intellect to produce enormous impact. She too found the speech so striking that she remembers both the occasion and the ideas with startling clarity. Such could rarely be said about the effect of any public speech.

She became for many people a symbol of British faith, a comfort to the confused. Her conservatism offended liberals, but satisfied a real need in the midst of anguish. Those who saw her at work were amazed at the ease and speed with which she could plan and present speeches. By now she had a secretary to do her typing for her; but she could dictate, without notes, a radio speech that would end precisely on the minute. When she timed it, she would tell her secretary to take out 50 words so that it would be perfect to the second. With her plays and speeches, she could know the applause and affection of her audience more directly than ever before. She warmed to the experience and developed into an increasingly dynamic and dramatic public figure. In her later days, she found the requests too frequent and began turning down the majority of them. But the Sayers papers on file at Witham and Wheaton testify to her zeal especially during the war years.

Since the speeches, broadcasts, and articles were usually by invitation, on an assigned topic or a burning issue of the moment, and since they were hastily constructed, one might expect these to be her most ephemeral work. But in fact a number of her essays and epigrams have been selected and republished since her death. They have stood the test of time and have withstood the more careful scrutiny of editors and scholars. Their relevance and sparkle remain undiminished after thirty years. Many feminists who never heard her voice have responded to her justly famous *Are Women Human?* as the almost perfect expression of a balanced Christian feminism that might have been written this morning. And many Christian artists and critics have found they can turn again and again to the outline for Christian art she introduced in "Towards a Christian Aesthetic" and developed in *The Mind of the Maker.* Her "Pantheon Papers," first published in *Punch,* with the "Calendar of Unholy & Dead-letter Days" is one of the funniest satires ever written on modern abuses of knowledge and worship. She notes the cult of appearance and perpetual youth, the adoration of woman for her physical attributes under The Beautification of St. Henna. The Venerable Bernard Shaw, that old master of words without faith, wit without hope, becomes the symbol of shallow intellectual and aesthetic pleasures that mirror the artist without shedding light onto the darkening world. St. Sigmund Sub-Limine is her attack on the new mythology of psychology that replaces the will with the twitch, the soul with glands. The Fiery Loins of St. Lawrence, D. H. pays proper tribute to the modern veneration of human sexuality. And St. Julian the Polymath is the symbol of modern adoration of science. St. Marx the Evangelist blesses his followers with the vain hope of the City of Man on earth. And all these modern unholy saints circle around the Apotheosis of the Common Man, standing with his rolled umbrella and pin-striped suit while angels play saxophones (Sayers is reported to have played a saxophone herself) and spotlights shine from above. She attacks ours as an age of cacophony, umbrage, and advertisement, celebrating progress, urbanity, and petrol. In the drawing and in her explanation of the new church year, its celebrations and services, she manages an extended, insightful jest at her world. (The papers were collected and reprinted by Roderick Jellema in *Christian Letters to a Post-Christian World*, 1969. This book was reprinted in 1978—but without Jellema's introduction and without the color plate—as *The Whimsical Christian: 18 Essays*.)

I am tempted to quote her ideas at length because so many of her phrases are such a delight. But there is no substitute for reading Sayers' work. Paraphrase does not hold a candle to the full experience of watching her develop an idea, surprise the reader/listener with her explication of a passage, display her marvelous command of tone, her caustic wit, her common sense, and her exceptional imagination.

Behind all of her work, as Lionel Basney has pointed out, there is a discernible pattern.[1] The foundations, as they have been through all her work, are primarily theological.

There were of course, in the war years, some words of encouragement and cheer to the British. Her patriotism was vigorous, but not blind. She criticized the cowardly rush of some English to the sanctuary of America, but then she also criticized the English response to

Wodehouse's so-called treason. She loved the British but was not inclined to see anyone as perfect. It is not surprising, with her deep love of her British heritage, that she should become an outspoken patriot in wartime. Even Lord Peter returned to write letters about proper ways to cross streets during blackouts and to note philosophic implications of the war. And then followed her advice on the proper use of both war and peace (*Creed or Chaos?* and *Begin Here*). Her experience in the business world led her briefly into economic exhortations which sound, despite her Tory leanings, suspiciously like Christian socialism. For the most part, in her social criticism, she attacked greedy capitalism and dictatorial communism both, seeking a path of economic virtue in self-discipline. She noted that it is difficult for the ordinary person to develop a "sacramental attitude to work, while many people are forced, by our evil standard of values, to do work which is a special degradation.[2] Her own love of work and belief in its power to enrich life led her to believe in its redemptive value in other lives. "Whatever your hand finds to do," says the Preacher, "do it with your might." (Eccles. 9:10) Having done this all of her life, she proposed it as a formula for others, a remedy for their lives of quiet desperation. By work, she did not mean simply writing. Workers around Witham recall that she was accustomed to watch them at work, ask questions about their tools and methods, and even suggest alternate ways of plumbing or digging or carpentering. She loved all kinds of labor and thoroughly enjoyed watching artisans at their craft. The happy worker she believed to be a happy person.

War she knew to be a temporary circumstance, one of the perennial results of sin. She never suggested that Britain deserved its pain. Witham was in the path of the bombing and experienced the daily bomb warnings along with London. But she did not see herself as an innocent victim. For herself, she asserted that she could not think of any personal misfortunes which had befallen her which were not, in one way or another, her own fault. At a time when other folk were "steeped in self-pity" this must have seemed a strong tack to take.[3]

In fact, Sayers brought gusto and laughter into adversity. During the shortages, she raised pigs (never more than one at a time) to provide pork, named "Francis Bacon" or "Fatima" depending on gender. She saw no reason to retreat into depression of spirit because of this national crisis. The sensible solution is to pull up your socks and get busy doing your bit.

It would have been an ideal time for the British government to use her services, and it apparently occurred to the Ministry of Information. She was summoned for an interview, but her appointment never went forward. Opposite her name on the files is the note "very loquacious and difficult."[4] The BBC frequently rejected her help as well, asserting that people preferred not to listen to a woman's voice and that her ideas were too doctrinal. But Sayers was accustomed to rejection and had learned to shake the dust off her feet and move along to the next town. She did not pause to lament their taste or to pity herself. Because of the war, and the consequent confrontation with the reality of death, people were eager to live without remembering why they live at all. Sayers sought a radical reconsideration of values, a rationale not for existence but for the abundant life. She had lived through World War I at Oxford and had lived through the aftermath in London; she feared a repetition of the cynicism and disillusionment that had followed that war. If anything, the emergence of the Nazi horror on the landscape should convince people that evil is real, immediate, and dangerous. The Romantic notion that people are good by nature is patently ridiculous. The Christian should not be surprised by beastly barbarism. She quotes Lord David Cecil on the relevance of original sin: " 'Christianity has compelled the mind of man, not because it is the most cheering view of human existence, but because it is truest to the facts.' "[5] Evil has not been cured by medicine, analyzed away by psychology, or cosmetically improved by wealth. The sacred doctrine of progress is clearly discredited by the fact of recurrent human barbarism.

Dorothy L. Sayers had the platform to make her statement about the world. She won a wide listening audience for her BBC broadcasts, her plays were well received and well attended, and crowds jammed into her public lectures. She was deeply involved in St. Anne's Church and in lectures in Soho. She chose to use her power to teach a theologically ignorant world the meaning of their creeds and to show them their relevance to their own lives. As she saw it, the world faced a choice, not between culture and anarchy, but between creed and chaos. No longer could Christians be vaguely on the side of social betterment or egocentrically concerned with emotional orgies. The church stood in need of "strong meat" for mature people, not the intellectual pap that had been satisfying them during their affluent days. Her work, as she saw it, was not to discuss her own personal religious experience or preach her social-economic doctrines, but to explicate the historical doctrines of the Christian church. Sayers had come to the recognition that her strength lay in her intellect, in her talent for teaching. But the teaching was not to a group of youngsters without experience or interest. Her role was that of schoolmistress to the multitudes. Her own imagination was harnessed to serve the tradition of the Christian church, and thereby to serve her Lord.

Most of her essays and speeches of the war years and after are explanations of certain favorite phrases in the Nicene Creed. She presented the history of the creed in *The Emperor Constantine*, and in other works did a careful phrase-by-phrase exegesis of it. But certain sections appealed to her so much that she worried them over in her mind, returning to them again and again. She loved especially the image of God the creator and the doctrine of the incarnation. These she used as the basis for her Christian aesthetic, her views on women, and her sacramental view of work. She had at last come to the experience of the "feeling intellect"—the mind married to the imagination and emotions in a mature reconsideration of the central ideas of her life.

"I believe in one God the Father almighty, maker of heaven and earth, and of all things visible and invisible." So opens the Creed, calling immediately to mind the whole of those first chapters of Genesis. God created this and that, and then he created a man—in his own image. We are by nature creative, as God is himself. God appears to Sayers as the supreme creative artist, the greatest of all makers. That aspect of us most nearly like God is our creativity. The artist, or human maker, like God, takes the materials at hand: clay, paint, experience itself, and out of these creates new life. Yet the manner in which the artist uses experience—or any other materials—transforms them. It is therefore irrelevant to worry over the events of an artist's life or emotions. Even if we dig them out, we cannot thereby explain (or explain away) the works of art. For the work is not the experience or the emotion, but an expression of it that becomes an experience itself. In fact, writers may not even know what their experience was until they write it, and in the writing put it into words, thereby recognizing the experience for what it is.[6] In so doing, writers achieve a mastery over their own past, no longer feeling battered victims of external events. This is certainly Sayers' own use of experience and of art. And her point is that by showing forth her experience in this new form, she makes something valuable of it, something that others may look at and recognize as their own experience as well. This is so much more than the original materials of art that the artist, like God, may be said to be making something out of nothing. The total is certainly far more than the sum of its parts.

This notion of God as artist solved for Sayers the problems posed in the centuries-old debate between science and religion. If Darwin was right in his notion of the origin of the world and its creatures, then Genesis would appear to be wrong. In *The Documents in the Case*, the scientists discuss the "breath of life" as the very element that is as yet unknown to science. Now Sayers carries her argument a step further by showing that a creative artist works differently from a scientist. The creative artist may start in the middle of existence, even planting a history and foreshadowing a future. Her fanciful explanation shows her very deep concern for this controversy that had shattered the faith of so many moderns. It does not seem to have convinced many listeners, but it did make her comfortable to believe that the war between science and faith had been grossly overstated.

Actually, Sayers was less concerned with constructing an argument to counter the evolutionists than she was at discovering the deeper truth of Genesis. She enjoyed Sir Arthur Eddington's differentiation of natural and normative law. She saw many of her own moral and aesthetic theories derived from a concern with what God created, not with what we think he should have created. As she explained the difference in *The Mind of the Maker*, the two kinds of law can be illustrated in the example of making an omelet. The law that eggs must be broken is a natural law—the way the universe is constructed. The law that the chef must wear a hat while making the omelet is a law of human opinion, not at all essential to the success of the omelet itself. Aristotle's laws are for the most part descriptive—laws that describe how art and morality work. They are discoveries, not creations. If we seek to violate them, we do not have an omelet or a work of art or a whole person.

Genesis tells only of the creation; our job has been to discover the nature of that creation and to use it wisely.

From this sense of the need to discover the innate rules, she is able to derive certain keys to art and to life. An artistic work must have unity, for example, or it does not please and does not survive. If we reject our own talents, our own work, our need to love our fellow creatures, we are not at peace with ourselves, with others, or with God. The Seven Deadly Sins are deadly not because the Catholic Church said so but because they are fatal distortions of our basic nature. If we allow ourselves to be slothful or greedy or envious, we are perverting our "image of God" and creating our own hell.

Bringing fresh and colorful insights to the "Other Six Deadly Sins," Sayers explains them in vivid modern terms. Predictably, sloth offends her more than most, for it is not simply a failure to do one's proper work, but also a failure to make moral judgments. The intellectual laziness of lukewarm Christians appalled her. Understandably, she thought lust a warmer and more forgivable sin than envy or wrath or greed. And she thought pride a very easy sin for the intellectual to slip into—the "last infirmity of noble mind." It is clear that her love of tradition and of the Middle Ages was drawing her closer to Catholicism, but her love of Britain kept her from affiliation with Rome. Her ideas, frequently derived from close and loving reading of the church fathers, were to reach their fullest development in the years she studied Dante—that work being the brilliant culmination of her meditation on sin and salvation.

"God created man in his own image . . . male and female he created them," says Genesis 1:27. This equal creation of woman as one branch of humanity, not a separate species and not secondary, delighted Dorothy L. Sayers. Woman, like man, was created in the image of God; and she was good. She too had then and still retains in her fallen nature the God-given creativity, the "desire and ability to make things." She too has her work in the garden of this world, and she too shares in the admonition to fill the earth and to subdue it.

Sayers fully appreciated the story of the fall and its dire effects. She believed in free will as essential for genuine love, and knew that such freedom allowed for sin as well as love. But sin she found a more comforting explanation of evil and a more helpful one than heredity or glands. Because Christians believe in free will, they believe people can change and seek forgiveness. The fall is not our fate but our free choice.

Since Adam and Eve did not eat of the fruit of the Tree of Life, they were faced with aging and death. Accepting Paul's declaration of Christ's victory over the grave, she had no reason to resent age or to fear death. She had never had occasion to worship at the temple of youth; and though she loved life, she believed that life everlasting awaited her behind the door of death. As she noted in her essay "Strong Meat," if we are to look forward, we must accept the values of aging.[7] To prefer youth is to spend most of our lives looking backward and envying others. This point she had illustrated in the grotesque old women pursuing their athletic young lounge lizards in *Have His Carcase*. For those of us entering the twilight years of our lives, when we shall never expect to be free again of bifocals and tired blood, it is indeed a comfort to know we are moving toward the "best of life." Certainly "maturity" sounds more attractive then "senility." Nor can death threaten us when we know that death itself has died in the victory of Christ.

"I believe . . . in one Lord Jesus Christ," says the Creed. Sayers saw the incarnation as the central miracle in human history—the greatest drama ever staged. Real God made himself a real man—fully human, fully divine, a miraculous blending of opposites in a single creature. Dorothy L. Sayers was enough of a scholar to know all the heresies and where they led. She rejected the Arian denial of Christ's divinity, the Gnostic and Docetic denial of his humanity. And she especially rejected the notion of "gentle Jesus meek and mild." She worshiped Christ, in his full divine humanity. Born of woman, therefore affirming the value of the flesh, he pointed clearly to the "affirmative way." Human life is itself of value, not simply to be endured but to be experienced fully. Her Christ lived human life richly, thereby redeeming existence from the life-in-death concept to a life of abundance. For Sayers, both religion and literature are valid only if they lead to an enriching of life: " 'I came that they may have life, and have it abundantly.' " (John 10:10) Christ turned water into wine, made the sick whole, raised the dead from the grave. Her hero in *The Man Born to*

Be King is a bringer of life, more glorious by far than his shadows Dionysus and Pan. He is an artist in his words, in his touch, and in his life.

In *The Mind of the Maker,* Sayers uses the person of Christ as the explanation of the central act of creativity. The Idea (God, the Father), has no material form until it becomes Energy (Christ, the Son) and then enters human hearts as Power (the Holy Spirit). The Son, then, as the material form of the Idea is parallel to the artifact, the making of the work out of words or clay or sound. Sayers saw art as a communication process, not a thing. Thus the original concept, the enfleshment of that concept, and the experiencing of it are all part of the whole. For the artist concerned solely with aesthetics, the work itself is the central value, an object of adoration. For more egocentric artists, ideas are what is paramount, even if they are never given shape. And for market-oriented artists, audience response is the final measure of their work. How many copies will it sell? How many people will go to see the movie? Will it be on the best-seller lists? For Dorothy L. Sayers, the work of art has life only if it is a strong idea moving from the mind of the creator into a separate and appropriate form and from thence to the mind and heart of the audience. This aesthetic keeps the Christian artist from idolatry: the worship of self, the work, or the marketplace.

It also gives a Christian artist the basis for judging a work of art. Among Sayers' most delightful discussions is that section of *The Mind of the Maker* she calls "Scalene Trinities." She equates each person of the Godhead and each part of the creative process with a side of an equilateral triangle. The exaggeration of any one side of this triangle throws the whole shape out of kilter. Her examples are vivid indeed, showing scalene triangles with excess of idea, or inordinate attention to form, or pandering to public taste. Then, in a fantastic surge of imagination, she demonstrates how artistic distortions parallel theological ones. Each is a form of heresy. She is one of the few authors who knows her theology so well she can play with it and make jokes out of heresies. Down under, she is deadly serious, but her surface sparkles with laughter.

Through this imaginative process, she constructs a mode of aesthetic evaluation which Christian critics can find quite useful. It is typical of Sayers that she would insist on the necessity of judgment. Her days in advertising had taught her the perils of the undiscriminating life. Christ did not smile benevolently on the just and the unjust alike. He hugged the little children and called the hypocrites "vipers" and "whited sepulchres." As Sayers noted, whatever else we can say about Christ, we can never say he was dull. It is the modern Christians with their lukewarm, nonjudgmental faith, their pious adherence to the "Seven Deadly Virtues" that have bored the modern world into a rejection of their dynamic Lord. If Christians are not ready to make evaluations of their world, then they are not ready to make choices in their lives. We let bad art into our churches and bad writing into our Sunday schools and praise mediocre performance rather than hurt somone's feelings. We do not give God our best, and we do not expect it of others. Sayers would see a significant difference between the quality of her play *The Man Born to Be King* and the rock musical *Jesus Christ Superstar*. She was willing to point out bad theology and shoddy work. She demanded high standards of herself and never hesitated to demand them of others. God's worker should do work worthy of the Master.

Among the reasons she loved Christ-the-man were his ties to the world of work. He was a carpenter who lived among common folk and called fishermen to his fellowship. He consorted with fallen women, drunks, and tax collectors—the sinners whom Sayers also knew and loved. He was a man who took pleasure in the same things she did: good food and good fellowship. He loved to use his words with precision; his epigrams are pithy and imaginative. He had insights others rarely have. He could laugh his disciples out of their petty arguments and see the perils of their individual strengths. He knew Judas to be so intelligent that he could be tricked by his own intelligence. He knew Peter's heart was right even when his will was confused. This is the Christ Sayers presented in *The Man Born to Be King*, one who offended many modern Britons as he had offended the ancient Pharisees.

Naturally she loved his behavior with women. As she notes in *Are Women Human?*, he never idealized, patronized, or condescended to women. He pointed out their sins to them. If they were mature enough to commit the sin, he considered them mature enough to handle the criticism. He welcomed them as followers and talked frankly with them about the faith, answering their questions about himself and his kingdom. He treated them as fully human. No wonder women were the last at the cross and first at the grave. They knew that he was unique:

"They had never known a man like this Man—there never has been such another."[8]

The climax of this most impressive of all human dramas was, she asserted, the miracle of Easter. God chose to become an actor in the play he had written, to assume the burden of the sins of the characters he had created, and to die for them. God is not only the author of all good and perfect gifts in life, he "is alive and at work *within* the evil and the suffering, perpetually transforming them."[9] Christian life is not an avoidance of pain or simply a cleansing through suffering. It is a redemption of pain by turning it to new use without ignoring the fact of its existence. We have a God who proved himself so loving as to experience human pain himself, who trod the same path we tread. Sayers herself had discovered that the Christian path is not protected and easy. Rather than escaping pain, the Christian must face it in hand-to-hand combat. With God's help, Christians have more than survival, they have victory. The resurrection is our final assurance that we are not mere animals spinning about witlessly on a blighted planet, but creatures of God, made by him for the purpose of fellowship with him.

In these essays, Dorothy L. Sayers drew on her personal experience, her literary scholarship, her wide reading in contemporary ideas, her theological studies, and her lively imagination. She played with ideas easily, combining quotations from Berdyaev and experiences with her cat; ideas from Sir Arthur Eddington and Aristotle were measured by her method of making an omelet. People admired the breadth and depth of her mind, but they loved her homey wit and realism.

Works of Apologetics and Education

1938	"The Greatest Drama Ever Staged" (also called "The Triumph of Easter")
	"Are Women Human?"
1939	*Strong Meat* (including the title essay and "The Dogma Is the Drama")
1940	"Creed or Chaos?"
	Begin Here: A War-Time Essay
1941	"The Other Six Deadly Sins"
	"The Mysterious English"
	"The Church in War's Aftermath"
	The Mind of the Maker
1942	"Why Work?" (address)
1945	"The Execution of God"
1947	*Unpopular Opinions* (essays)
	Creed or Chaos? (essays)
1957	"Christian Belief About Heaven and Hell"

Posthumous

1969	*Christian Letters to a Post-Christian World*, ed. Roderick Jellema (reprint of selected essays; reissued 1978 as *The Whimsical Christian: 18 Essays*)
1971	*Are Women Human?* (including the title essay and "The Human-Not-Quite-Human")
1973	*A Matter of Eternity*, ed. Rosamond Kent Sprague (excerpts)

VII. *The Celestial City*

When she was a child, Dorothy Sayers dreamed of returning to Oxford. When she became a teenager, she found a home there for her disinterested love of scholarship. Whenever she returned, she found the same sense of Oxford as the "still centre where the spinning world Sleeps on it axis."[1] When asked years later to return as a speaker, she told her audience that they must never transform Oxford into a "rich boys' playground," but must always keep it the "poor scholar's workshop." When Harriet Vane went back for her Gaudy Night, she too dreamed of leaving the busy life of the popular novelist for the quiet scholarship of Oxford. There she might finally do a work of real value, one with no advertising potential, but one of which the critic might say, "Miss Vane has handled her subject with insight and accuracy." Ironically, the scholarship Sayers planned on Collins was never finished and the novel she considered her tribute to her love of scholarship, *Gaudy Night*, won her instead the permanent hostility of the dons at Somerville College. They saw themselves mercilessly satirized in the various portraits. Dr. Barbara Reynolds, a Cambridge lecturer in Italian, has noted those characteristics Sayers most cherished in Oxford, and those she felt Oxford had cultivated in her: the scholar's habit of orderly thinking, the precise use of words, and the sense of pleasure in sharing knowledge.[2] She thought Oxford the home of those who loved learning for its own sake, and she believed it should be preserved for such people.

But Oxford, for all of her love and her occasional visits, was not really home for Sayers, any more than the temporary gathering of actors in a theater was a lasting community. Her city was to be a different one. Her community was never to be the community of scholars, in spite of her deep and lasting love for her Oxford friends. She continued to correspond with former teachers; she was delighted by her cordial relationship with the Inklings—especially Charles Williams and C. S. Lewis. And she became close friends with Dr. Reynolds, a younger scholar who worked with her in her last years. But her path was too different, her career too checkered to adjust completely to those whose lives had been more placid, less varied. She could visit the world of scholars, but she was not content to live there exclusively.

She had never abandoned her love of languages and of the Middle Ages. Those first years, while working at advertising and at mystery writing, she was also publishing her translation of *Tristan.* She sought to justify her stories of detection by presenting them as modern romances, making Lord Peter as heroic as she dared. Later, her chancel dramas drew heavily on medieval sources. *The Man Born to Be King* had close parallels in the English mystery plays. Still remembering the encouragement of the fine scholar Mildred Pope, she finally completed her work on the translation of *The Song of Roland.* The lucid and lively introduction to this work is a model of scholarship, blending rich learning, contemporary commentary, and realism with her usual touch of wit. She had drawn heavily on Thomistic thought for her aesthetic ideas in *The Mind of the Maker,* and had based the entire book on insights from St. Augustine.

She loved the medieval world for its architecture, its music, its languages, and its religion. Like Eliot, she saw in medieval thought a "unified sensibility" that had been eroded in the Renaissance. Although fragmentation had gradually become the key to modern thought, Sayers sought to reconstruct for herself and for others a unity of all learning, feeling, and faith. She did not accept the modern notion that science and religion belong in different segments of the brain, that popular culture must be separated from traditional culture, that the scholar cannot be a part of the commercial world. Hers was by nature and by temperament as unified a sensibility as any medieval saint ever knew—a unity, however, not granted by birth, but won by effort.

She had not studied Italian as one of her numerous languages, and therefore had not been inclined to study Dante. Although her friend Charles Williams had recommended him to her and had finally written a book on Dante's imagery (*The Figure of Beatrice*), Dorothy L. Sayers had hesitated to approach this old master she pictured "steeped to his eyebrows in grimth."[3] She did have a copy of *The Divine Comedy* in the house, and it came to hand one night during an air raid. While she and her husband huddled with others in the air-raid shelter waiting for the all clear, she started on her final great adventure. She was so thrilled with Dante's approach, his ideas, his world, his poetry, and his religion that she felt a deep friendship with this medieval Italian master. In the surge of power that filled her across the centuries, she knew she must be his interpreter for the modern world.

At the time he composed his *Commedia*, Dante Alighieri of Florence was a middle-aged man, in the middle of the journey of his life. He had come from a proud and wealthy family, was well educated and active in the politics of his town, had some small popularity in literary circles as a result of his impassioned love lyrics. He was married, with four or more children, and was a comfortable member of the Florentine upper class. Suddenly, he found his life and thoughts thrown into confusion. After a lifetime of being a loyal citizen of his town, devoted to its ideals and activities, serving on its governing board and traveling as its envoy, he returned to Florence to find himself an exile, charged with fraud and corruption, forbidden entry to his beloved city unless he was willing to be "burned with fire till he be dead."[4] His wife and children, dreading his fate, chose to remain in the sanctuary of the city where they could have the protection of her prestigious family and friends. "Thou shalt leave everything beloved most dearly; this is the first shaft which the bow of exile lets fly," he wrote of himself.[5] For the rest of his life, twenty long years, this lonely wanderer was to climb other men's stairs and eat the salt at other men's tables. Loving and wealthy patrons proved generous to him, but he never was able to return to the mainstream of his life. He carried with him apparently scant but ample baggage: his anger, his love, his great talent, and his faith.

Certainly Dorothy L. Sayers had also found herself in the middle of her life to be lost in the hell of loneliness, indignation, and disappointment. Her compensation, like Dante's, lay in the gradual exploration of the hell of self through the stages of renewal to the ecstasy of the vision of God. Dante's legacy to the world is the complex and beautiful record of this marvelous journey of faith, which has come to be known as *The Divine Comedy.* Dorothy L. Sayers' legacy is the translation, explication, and "showing forth" of this work.

Her preparation for this work, in spite of her gap in Italian studies, was almost perfect. She had established the meticulous habits essential for good scholarship and was willing to take time to explore the minutiae with zeal and care. Dr. Reynolds, who was Sayers' choice as the translator to complete the unfinished portion of the *Paradiso,* testifies to her working through as many as ten or twelve different translations of a passage, discussing the merits of each, and choosing the best on a rational and aesthetic basis. She was willing to follow Dante through his experimentation with mirrors, to explore falconry or cosmology or second causes as they became necessary to understand the text. Like Charles Williams, she believed translators should be vehicles for knowledge, not artists asserting their own identities and eccentricities or calling attention to their own discoveries. The translator should have Keats' "negative capability," the ability to efface oneself in the experience of the other. While the arrogant scholar prefers to twist the meanings of the authorities, seek out strange and esoteric meanings, and adjust evidence to fit private ends, the true scholar will try to see the truth shining through the words. The scholar, unlike the advertiser, has a first obligation to the discovery and communication of the truth. In her scholarship, Sayers had finally found a solution to all the anger she had felt at listening to journalists, lawyers, and copywriters twist words to fit their private purposes.

The morality of the scholar was very important to Dorothy L. Sayers. Scholarship, she had always suspected, was the work she was set on earth to do. At last, enabled to do her proper work, she did it with all her heart. In her sacramental approach to her work, she believed that the linguist was called upon to study the original text, to translate it as precisely and as beautifully as possible, and to establish thereby a new creation in harmony with the stylistic and philosophic qualities of the original.

If, however, the audience is separated from a work by centuries of changing interest, increasing specialization, scientific discoveries, reformed religion—the myriad alterations attending the Renaissance and Reformation—then the task of the scholar is to explain, to interpret, and to relate the work of art in its context to readers in theirs. For such a task, the translator must have a wide understanding of contemporary history and thought as well as vast learning in the medieval culture. To avoid pedantry, the translator must have thought enough about life to see the continuing elements in human existence and to relate details to these. Such knowledge and wisdom and insight can come only from experience, study, and meditation. Dorothy L. Sayers was therefore wise indeed to have approached Dante in the middle of the journey of her own life, prepared by a full life for the arduous task of study and the imaginative leap of understanding.

As Dr. Reynolds so beautifully expressed the situation:

> In 1943 Charles Williams' book *The Figure of Beatrice* is published. This makes her resolve to read Dante. But some months go by before she does. We now from our point of perspective can see into her future. We move her along the line of time to the summer of 1944. We place her now in our mind in the air raid shelter in her garden here in Witham, physically in the very midst of destructive forces, and bring her face to face with Dante.
>
> I said that the moment, the summer of 1944 and the age of 51, was of paramount significance. You can see now what I meant by that. It was a moment of intersection in her own life. Her intellect, her reading, had reached a peak of maturity. She had been thinking thoughts and contemplating concepts which belonged to the same universe as Dante's. It was a moment of crisis for her country, for the Western world and for Christendom.[6]

Sayers had discovered that certain work can be done properly only if one has prepared for it—even if the preparation has been unconscious. The scattered bits of her life fell into a meaningful pattern at last. Linguistic skill and intellect had always been her strengths. She prided herself on her ability to bring her head and her hand to a job with combined zeal and power. But Dante demanded her heart as well.

She always suspected that she was too cerebral to be a true Christian. Paul had told the Corinthians that the gospel was foolishness to the Greeks, and in some ways Dorothy Sayers was a good Greek—and a bad Christian. Even when quoting the gifts of the Spirit, she sneaked one addition of her own into the Scripture: not only faith, hope, and love, but the good of the intellect.[7] Her pride in her own exceptional mind and her trust in intellectual truth sometimes warped her writing, leaving it cold and rational and slightly blighted by the chill. But in Dante, she found the intellect joined with the heart and the soul to allow the full experience of Christian faith—a proper use for all her heart, and all her strength, and all her mind.

One of the remarkable qualities of Sayers was her ability to open herself to new experiences and to continue growing. At an age when other women believe their best years are behind them, Sayers was rejoicing in the maturity that gave her fresh insights into an old master and delighting in her own new growth and experimentation. To live for her was to learn, to experience, to enjoy. She never settled for what she had already accomplished, always looked eagerly forward to her next adventure. This is a Christian romanticism, delighting in each new moment. It is quite different from pagan romanticism, holding to the past and to youthful thrills—the moment that the youth reaches for the maiden and the maiden is almost caught. The ecstasy of passion depends on the age and health of the body. The ecstasy of the spirit knows no such prison. When the mind, the heart, and the spirit dominate life, the fading body is not the end of hope or joy.

Charles Williams had known all along that Dorothy Sayers would find a compatible mind in Dante. He was right. She was delighted with *The Figure of Beatrice* (for Charles Williams was, in many ways, as intellect-oriented as she), and with her final plunge into the work of the master. While she had expected to meet in Dante a "superhuman sourpuss," she found instead a man who can tell a good story, laugh at himself, and enjoy the fullness of human life.[8] As a writer of novels, she could admire his architectonic design, his careful adumbration of incident, his orderly yet varied method, his precise use of realistic detail, and his ability to wring a plausible solution out of a seemingly impossible situation. As a medievalist, she enjoyed his meshing of classical and Scholastic ideas, his transformation of medieval romance, his adaptation of classical epic to medieval form, his imaginative use of vernacular and literary speech, his passionate excitement about history and ideas. And as a Christian, she could enjoy his understanding of sin and his experience of salvation. She says she loved him for his ideas—the ordered, hierarchical, rational, purposeful vision of the universe—for his feeling intellect, for his preference for the Way of Affirmation, for the brilliance of his style, and for the grandeur of his scope. Perhaps more than any of these, she loved him because she shared his religion. Dorothy L. Sayers experienced Dante as a real person, full of vitality, love, anger, excited by life, sensitive to every moment and part of it. He had a rich awareness of full humanity that spoke powerfully to her.

She says that friends "endured" her mania for "the *Comedy* with sympathetic interest rather than whole-hearted answering enthusiasm."[9] Cut off from this immediate form of communication, she turned to speeches, papers, and letters, especially to a few old friends and a few new ones who did share her zeal.

Sayers, like C. S. Lewis, was a great letter writer. For her, letters were like conversation, full of laughter, details of daily life, insights, and interests. She found that her life expanded as she reached out to others through her letters.

In the last decade of her life she was a great traveler too, visiting friends, checking libraries, and making speeches. Fleming complained about her absence, but could not satisfy her hunger for good talk and good company. When he died, she seems to have found herself relieved of a central worry in her life, but too drained to enjoy her freedom. She tried to renew the old delight by taking a walking trip with friends, but something had gone out of her.

Among those who mattered especially to Dorothy Sayers in her last years were the Inklings. They had all long been in love with the Middle Ages, and both C. S. Lewis and Charles Williams had explored aspects of the courtly-love tradition. Her moving tributes to Williams after his death show especial affection and admiration. Through the speeches she made at Cambridge, Sayers met someone who was to become a close and lifelong friend—Dr. Barbara Reynolds, a scholar in Italian literature and language who had already translated Ariosto and was at work on an Italian-English dictionary. With these and others, this aging zealot was able to establish a temporary community of like minds that responded to her letters and enjoyed her discussions of ideas, words, phrasing, and problems of translation.

Unlike too many senior citizens, she found people enjoyed her because she was so full of life. Dr. Reynolds tells of her pleasure in talking well into the night, occasionally so delighted with an idea or expression that she would laugh until she cried. She was great fun to be with, never stuffy or snobbish or worried about the opinion of others. Her curiosity and enthusiasm kept her from any temptation to settle into the classic trap of rheumatic pettiness that makes aging such a bore. When she felt unwell, she disappeared to her room until she recovered, never burdening others with her frailties. She apparently refrained from complaining about conditions at home with her husband except on rare occasions.[10] Hers was the practical mind-set that one should complain only about those issues that have remedies. If she could argue a point with an erring bishop via the *Times*, thereby correcting his logic or theology as well as muffling his voice, she would rip off a letter immediately. She relished the liveliness of a theological battle, which could be fought logically on the issues, but never a personal argument, which was seldom based on rules of logic or clearly defined rational issues.

She refused to burden others with her declining health. James Brabazon notes that she despised "doing herself good," by such modern foolishness as exercise and diet. Rather than complaining about her declining energies and her poor circulation, she found a new focus for her interests and sought out like-minded people. She had noted some years earlier in her speech at the Oxford Union, "It is a simple fact that the brain (commonly speaking) outlasts both the body and the emotions, so that it is rare indeed for a scholar to outlive his own interests and usefulness."[11]

An even richer explanation of her vitality is provided by the Reverend Aubrey Moody, who recalls taking Dorothy Sayers, Sybil Thorndike and Lewis Casson to dinner at a little restaurant in Soho. Suddenly he noticed the quiet as everyone in the place listened to these "two great women" talking. As he explains it:

> Sybil Thorndike once told me that every morning when she woke up she would say to herself, "O good, another day, and I am going to learn

> something new." In one of her essays Dorothy Sayers, after quoting the words of Christ—"Except ye become as little children"—said, "You can wake on your fiftieth birthday with the same forward-looking excitement and interest in life that you enjoyed when you were five." "Except ye become as little children ye cannot see the kingdom of God." "One must not only die daily," she says, "but every day one must be born again."

She lived every day as if she believed with him, "Today is the first day of the rest of my life." It is a thrilling and thoroughly Christian motto, that looks hopefully forward to life and considers death a triviality.[12]

Among those new friends she developed were the "neo-medievalists," a group loosely united by their delight in the medieval synthesis. In a world that applauded Huxley's brave new world of plastic values or reveled in the aesthetic world-weariness of the nihilists, these scholars seemed quaint and quixotic. But theirs was not the simplistic denial of complexity; rather it was a hard-won Christian affirmation. C. P. Snow had lamented the grotesque split into two cultures, but C. S. Lewis sought to reunite them. In the medieval world, the ties of community, faith, and knowledge were clearer. These brilliant scholars and artists accepted the challenge of searching for a new synthesis for the modern world. Among these folk, Sayers was developing her Oxford-of-the-mind, which like the universal church is a spiritual rather than a physical reality, a communion that transcends time and space.

These fellow seekers shared with Dorothy L. Sayers a unified sensibility and a neo-medieval world view. Dante's world was held together by love: God's love led him to create the universe and to place us in it. For the medieval mind, and to a certain extent for Sayers as well, this universe was a three-storied one, with God as the unmoving mover of the heavens and the earth. Dante's religion was also his cosmology, his geography, and his physics. In a thrillingly cohesive vision of God's creation, he considered love as the key to all attraction, mental, physical, and spiritual. Thus, love of evil and of the material stuff of creation draws us deeper down into Hell, a place frozen and dark because of the absence of God's love, where the fallen gnaw at their fellows, mutilate them, lie to them, snarl at them: a place dominated by that lord of hate, Satan. God does not need to place people in their proper sphere of Hell; love for a particular evil draws each of them to it, to spend eternity repeating, without joy or hope, the sins each loved on earth.

But the person who loves Christ rather than Satan moves instead to the sunlit home of penitents—Purgatory. There the penitent eagerly seeks the whip and the bridle, finding the one an encouragement to virtue, the other a restraint from vice. Again, each person's faith and failure determine each one's abode in the afterlife. Since on earth love was divided between wrongful objects and rightful ones, each Christian sinner settles first in the place where the particular sin is to be confessed and cleansed. Living with both night and day, the rhythms of the earth, the sinners are gradually cleansed of their sins, growing lighter and brighter and more joyful as they approach purity and holiness. The rhythm of labor and rest, the sense of movement upward, the life of song, prayer, and penitence seem idyllically monastic. They are in startling contrast to the static despair of Hell.

Though Sayers' Protestant readers are likely to reject the literal existence of Purgatory and its attendant doctines, they will find her notes on Dante useful as a statement of the problems and potentials of life on earth. Her insights into the psychology and theology of sin, derived principally from Dante and his antecedents, include her own very lively awareness of the sins in the world. Therefore, her explanatory notes on sin, particularly pride and lust, are especially insightful.

The organization of Purgatory, like that of Hell, is based on the Seven Deadly Sins. As might be expected, Purgatory's highest point parallels Hell's; for in Dante's natural history, Purgatory was formed when Satan fell to the earth and displaced a great cone-shaped mass. Hell was the result of the impact and the shrinking of matter from his evil. The displaced land rose up to form the seven-story mountain. Though Sayers could not expect her audience to accept Dante's literal narrative, she knew they could enjoy it on a mythic and symbolic level. Psychologically as well as physically, Purgatory is the counterpart of Hell. Thus, while Hell is founded on despair and hatred of God, Purgatory is based on hope and the love of God. It is an image of the Christian life. Trusting God's ability to cleanse and forgive us, we may confront even our deepest sins with assurance. Thus Purgatory is a place of movement toward God and of mutual support among believers, where people openly admit their failures and praise the saints, who provide them with examples of Christian piety. Here they praise God, who gives them the faith and hope to change their lives.

The key to the ordering of the sins in Purgatory is distorted love. Dorothy L. Sayers, who had spent the early years of her life searching for love, spent the last years studying, interpreting, and translating Dante's great vision of it. In this man's work, she found the answers she had been seeking and had tried so hard to verbalize in one book after another. Her goal was to make this masterpiece accessible to English readers and to provide them the epiphany—the showing forth—she had had in reading it. Her hope for them was that they might not merely understand but that they might also feel the full joy of being awakened to the meaning for their own life.

The lower section of Purgatory, where the proud, the envious, and the wrathful do their appropriate penance, is the farthest from primal innocence, for here love is perverted. Those who should love their neighbors, love instead their neighbors' harm. Middle Purgatory, where the slothful compensate for their lives by racing toward perfection, is the home of defective love—those whose lukewarm love kept them from exertion for the love of God. Nearest to innocence are the covetous, the gluttonous, and the lustful. Their flaw is the love of God's creation rather than of God himself. The drunkard, the miser, and the fornicator ignore the primary good while desiring instead the secondary goods. But the lustful soul is the closest to purity because lust is the warmest of sins. The lustful can transfer their love of the flesh into a delight in the incarnation far more easily than the prideful can change their love of self into love of God. At least the lustful have turned their ideas toward other human beings, albeit with the wrong intent. Lust can turn to love, and love of humans can be altered to love of God.

The long years of worrying over love came to a final resolution in Dante. The early poems, the detective stories, and the plays had all touched on the fundamental human need for love. Now, in Dante, Sayers found a way to order and shape her own experience. She had known that lust was wrong, that perverse love can be destructive, that possessive love can stunt the lover and the beloved. Dante put all these experiences together into his own journey, which in so many ways paralleled her own.

Dante uses the medieval Roman Catholic understanding of sin and psychology of repentance. He pictures the public confession of sin (which Sayers had so self-consciously avoided), the repentance (contrition), the penance (satisfaction), explaining that each step is necessary to the cleansing process. Sayers' lucid explanation of the psychology of sin which is involved in this process makes sense of the formula which, without this breath of life, might appear an empty form.

She must have found herself speculating on whether she should have confessed her sins openly. Confession has the effect of cleansing that places the communicant back into a right relationship with God and his community. Hiding a sin allows it to fester, increases the guilt and hostility and fear. One wonders whether Sayers regretted the public person that masked the private self. She had carefully justified the artist's privacy, relying on the formalist's argument that one should trust the work, not the one who made it. But that is not the same as the pilgrim's forthright sharing of personal experience to make the way easier for fellow Christians. To admit error is to encourage others to share and to grow as well. First shame, then pride can keep us from telling the truth to an unsympathetic and censorious world. We can certainly understand anyone's reluctance to face a self-righteous public. But the age-old ritual of confession, contrition, and penance has a wholesome, cleansing effect. Sayers acknowledged the need for the ritual but rejected the public setting for it. She had nothing but contempt for public confession, preferring to preach the value of the doctrine rather than muddying the water with private experience.

She noted that she was primarily a classicist, a poet of statement, writing to tell what she knows.[13] She uses her experience as the basis for reaffirmation of various great truths, displaying a "mature" method by universalizing her individual discovery of truth. The more popular modern pattern is to involve readers in the individual's search rather than just hand them a map one has already traveled. She is not an evangelist or a seeker, but an explicator who has found her truth.[14] In a sense, as Dr. Reynolds has noted,[15] she always had the "congenital disease" of translating—a need to translate ideas, terms, experiences, and concepts for an ignorant and hungry contemporary audience.

Though Purgatory mountain itself seems to stand physically in time, the journey up it from sin to salvation, the return to innocence with the aid of the redeeming love of Christ, the gradual shedding of the burden of sin, the increasing sense of joy, and the freeing of the will through submission to Christ—all of these elements of the journey are timeless and universal. As Dante studies each of our sins and tries to discover its root causes, he acknowledges his own sins and bows his head in confession of his own pride and lust. His delight in redemption and renewal at the top of Mt. Purgatory is a thrilling moment. He invites each of us to explore each sin and to search our own hearts for traces of it.

His translator's full discussions of the sins suggest that Dorothy Sayers took time to imitate Dante by looking into her own life and heart and admitting each of the sins she found. Notes are not an appropriate mode for personal reference, but the insightfulness of her discussions testifies to her soul-searching. Lust and pride are her primary sins, as they were Dante's. She must have loved him all the more for confessing down the centuries sins she whispered to herself and to God.

It is in the Earthly Paradise that Dante comes face to face, at last, with his earthly love, Beatrice. Having experienced the forgiveness of sin and the forgetfulness of it, remembering only the thrilling experience of God's forgiveness, he emerges cleansed by the flame to face the Beatrician Pageant. This scene bears strong parallels to love as portrayed in Sayers' novels and conforms perfectly to her notion of the culminating human experience as mutual love between members of the opposite sex.

Heaven is also portrayed as a place of love, where the saints of the Church Triumphant live in the radiant presence of God. Here at last they see "face to face," knowing the truth, remembering no part of earthly life with regret, loving fully without the need to possess either things or people. In the light of God's love, their vision is restored so that they can see all things in their proper place and love them in their proper way. The nine spheres, each with its own planet, its supervising angels, and its human inhabitants, are all in actuality contained in the mind of God. Finally, all images break through in Paradise so that they live outside of time and space. Though the saints seem to be in various spheres, these are only metaphors. They all in fact dwell in the presence of God, in the *primum mobile*, flying like bees in and out of the Rose of the Blessed, in the glorious light of God's love. In a blinding moment, Dante finally experiences God and admits that his mystic moment is ineffable: his art cannot record the truth:

> Thither my own wings could not carry me,
> But that a flash my understanding clove,
> Whence its desire came to it suddenly.
>
> High phantasy lost power and here broke off;
> Yet, as a wheel moves smoothly, free from jars,
> My will and my desire were turned by love,
>
> The love that moves the sun and the other stars.[16]

This divine love that Dante experiences so richly takes different forms for him, as it does for each of us. His art is his own loving response to God, as Sayers' translation is her loving response to both God and to this master craftsman. Those activities, artifacts, people, or experiences to which we are inexplicably drawn are our "loves." Our need to garden or to cook or to write or to jog or to read or to sing or to compute or to preach is our magnetic force—that pull which is like gravity. Our love draws us to act, demands that we satisfy it until we can rest. Good gifts are the ones that help us to move upward, for they are from God. The sinful urges, which cannot be satisfied and which provide no rest but only new desire and disgust, pull us downward toward the hell of self and Satan. Christians must use their gifts, recognizing that God is the giver of all good and perfect gifts. They must never turn to worship the gift rather than the giver; nor should they use the gift in perverse ways. They should admire neither the gift nor themselves for having it, but turn to use it for God, delighting in his service. This is the message of Dante and of his translator. The beauties of this world, the talents that we have, are to be used for the greater glory of God.

Dante's love of other artists (especially Vergil), like Sayers', is not idolatry of secondary goods, but the pleasure in recognizing God's image shining through human work. Dante so identified his love of God and his love of beauty that he organized his "divine comedy" on the basis of the trinity—three in one. The three parts of the poem, the divisions within the poem, the complex threefold interlocking verse form (*terza rima*) all testify to his delight in the majesty and unity of God's threefold nature. Dorothy L. Sayers also felt that God's nature shows itself in our nature, and we respond with delight to those things which come closest to our own sense of the image of God imprinted on us. Her idea of the trinity of creativity reflects this faith that, if God is triune, we reflect his nature in our own creative acts. If God's triune nature is imprinted in us—who are created in his image—then her idea makes sense. We respond to the triune nature of art (Idea, Energy, and Power) because it mirrors our inmost nature. We love that art which expresses our truth—the goodness of God's creation, the reality of our fall, the glory of our redemption through Christ. For Sayers and for Dante, art is a record of human experience, an effort to communicate ideas, not a charming nonsense game played with paint and words.

Dante's love of other people also parallels Sayers'. She often found that other people opened up life for her in extremely rich ways. Charles Williams she found particularly delightful; his ideas "intoxicated" her. Alzina Stone Dale notes that Sayers met Williams in 1938, and occasionally came by to meet him at work (the offices of the Oxford University Press). They would go off to a wine bar together and talk for hours about religion and literature. After his death, she continued to correspond with his wife and children, showing continuing concern for those he had loved.[17]

Because she loved certain friends, they drew her along to new ideas and helped her to new discoveries. For her, life was a pilgrimage of love. Love of father had drawn her to love of language and love of church. Love of friends drew her to new authors and forms. The deepest experience of human love, the love between the sexes, she had known on occasion, as Dante had. And she found in certain friends a special image of God, drawing her not to themselves but through their love to the love of God. These folks she called "God-bearers." In Dante's life, Beatrice served as a God-bearer in a parallel manner. Using the frame of reference provided by his age to explain his experience and his emotions, he discovers in the image of Beatrice a means of access to the love of God. Her intervention for him, her prayers on his behalf, her delight in his redemption culminate in her appearance at the top of Mt. Purgatory, where she crowns him as his own pope and emperor, a free man in Christ, who is now: "Pure and prepared to leap up to the stars."[18]

Beatrice was the image that Charles Williams had pointed out for special notice in the poem. Of course, as a woman looking back over the centuries at another woman, far removed in context and experience, Dorothy Sayers found Beatrice fascinating. Sayers had long contemplated the significance of her own sexual identity and had decided that the popular religious traditions concerning women were for the most part a departure from the teachings and actions of Christ. The lady of the courtly-love tradition, Dante's tradition (that is the unlikely source of our own notions of pedestals and romance), was herself a curious distortion of the women in Scripture. The Gospels do not even hint at a need to venerate the virgin Mary or to idealize womanhood. The woman images in Revelation are certainly not meant as literal figures. The troubadours, developing a pagan mystique out of idolatrous and adulterous love, elaborated a code in which a man took his orders from his "lady," a creature of heavenly beauty and grace. Dante supposedly lived and died longing for Beatrice's favor; while in his actual life, his wife and daughters took orders from him and were little better than his servants. In her introductory notes on *Purgatorio,* Sayers explored this curious double path of courtly love and uncourtly life and sought to discover the reality of the woman beneath the trapping of words. She wanted to understand why Dante chose to use the complex figure of Beatrice in his poem, citing as his paramount redemptive human figure not his wife (Gemma Donati), but his lady. In doing so, he was obliged to transform a simple Florentine maiden into a guide who would serve as a bridge between the rational-aesthetic Vergil and the theological-spiritual St. Bernard. Her position and her ability to initiate and empower make Beatrice the central figure in understanding Dante.

Dorothy L. Sayers became convinced that, in Beatrice, Dante wrought the transvaluation of courtly love to a plane on which it made "profound spiritual sense." Dante, she noted, was of an age so saturated by the "Image of the Lady" that he was already "charged with the values of honor and courtesy and gentlehood, obedience and faith, solace and joy and devotion" before he ever saw Beatrice.[19] The age gave him a frame for his vivid personal experience.

He had written a mystical love journal entitled *La Vita Nuova* documenting the few encounters he had with the divine Beatrice, but nothing in the events of his life indicates that he was unfaithful to his wife or unhappy with her. The fact that his wife and children did not accompany him into exile from Florence could easily be accounted for in numerous ways besides a failure of love. And anyway, by then, the divine Beatrice had married a banker and had died. Her influence on Dante survived only in a remembered image of glorious womanhood. Yet she was a literal person, a real woman.

She was the "same Florentine girl who made fun of Dante at a party, who once cut him in the street, whose mere presence in the same city with him filled him with inexplicable anguish and ecstasy."[20] The literalness of the girl was enormously important to Sayers because it pointed to an affirmation of physical reality. Beatrice's beauty is a physical beauty at the beginning, and Dante delighted in the "body of glory" that Beatrice had on earth, thereby honoring the "holy and glorious flesh" which like all material things is to the Christian sacramental and symbolic of divine glory.[21] Dorothy L. Sayers did not have to be a beautiful woman, as the world understood beauty, to appreciate physical beauty and the value of this world's delights. She asserted, along with Charles Williams, her firm faith in the Way of Affirmation, the opposite of the ascetic's Way of Negation. This to her seemed enormously important, because the Way of Affirmation affirms the ingrained reasonableness of the universe, the validity of our senses and our reason. It affirms that art itself has value so long as it is true to its own standards, and that "the whole man, flesh and mind and spirit, is by his nature *capax Dei*—capable of God."[22] No one is submerged totally into another, nor even into the divine. The individual identity is significant. And images are also important, as the means by which we approach God. Thus, she concluded her beautiful tribute to Williams and to Dante,

> the way of Man lies through the streets of the City, through Florence or through London, through the Republic or through the Empire, to that one City of which we are all citizens, "the Rome," says Dante, "Where Christ is a Roman." And there, having with an ordered love adored all the types, we shall be permitted to look upon the Archetype—the Image within the Godhead, which by taking up of the images into itself is also—again in Dante's words—"dyed with our image."[23]

To have lived and loved so fully, to have worked so hard at her life and her art, Sayers needed the confirmation that this had all meant something. Dante believed it did, Charles Williams agreed, and Sayers was inclined to believe that they were right. The life of the ascetic, withdrawn from temptation, from the dust and sweat of the race, was not her way to God. The denial of the senses, with all of their pleasure in music and poetry and food and wine and sun and rain, would be a denial of God's good creation—good even though in a fallen state. Our senses may have distortions, but they are the means by which, along with our minds and hearts, we apprehend our kinship with God, the one who made this kinship for his pleasure and ours. This does seem to be ratified by the incarnation, the act by which God once again stepped into human history and chose to enter the flesh and live the life of dust and pain. Not only would the Way of Negation deny art, it would deny the validity of Christ's experience in the world.

But the experience of flesh was only the first step for both Sayers and Dante. Like him, she loved the Platonic Ladder of Love, a ladder whose lowest rung touched firmly to the earth, and whose highest entered heaven. She had no need to pull that ladder up after her as she ascended to her final resting-place. She liked knowing that the earth was there still, and she shared with Dante a solid satisfaction in realism as the basis for mysticism.

As we watch the various appearances of the God-bearer Beatrice through the story, we come to understand that she is not simply the beautiful wife of a Florentine banker who stirred and haunted Dante. She becomes instead a human form through which God speaks to the young man and encourages him to love more than the flesh, to climb the Platonic Ladder of Love to a higher love than lust alone can ever know. Because Dante loved this woman passionately and instinctively and without diminution (even when she married and later died), she becomes for him the very image of human love. Dorothy L. Sayers notes that love is a natural and fundamental human instinct. We were ourselves created in love and freed to love, and love is the motivating force in most of our lives. This basic instinct (*amor naturale*) draws us to whatever is good or pleasing; it may easily emphasize the senses and take us into the dark recesses of eros or on the other hand emphasize our rationality and draw us to *amor d'animo*. It may be nothing more than the perfunctory debt of love legally binding husband and wife (see Sayers' introduction to *Purgatory*, p. 13) or the wild frenzy of love drawing adulterous lovers to their doom (Tristan and Isolde). Dante divides Purgatory into categories of love, sees Hell as the absence of God's love, and envisions Paradise as a symphony of love moving upward toward God.

In her appearance in the Earthly Paradise, Beatrice becomes the image of the church, which encourages us to leave our limited loves for the immortal love of Christ. Like a good wife—the Bride of Christ—she nags man out of his preference for the physical to a love of the spiritual. Her admonitions shame, and her love heals. She seems like a good mother as much as a good wife, warning her erring children, encouraging them, laughing gently at their confusions, helping each of them toward the next stage of development.

With Beatrice as his guide, Dante bursts into Paradise. There, in the presence of the saints, he discovers insights into theological truths. With each sphere, Beatrice grows more beautiful, her smile more brilliant, until she finally must turn from her poet for fear of blinding him. As divine illumination floods into Dante's life, Beatrice becomes (in Sayers' phrase) a "divine schoolmistress," leading, explaining, protecting, nudging, hinting, helping the learner to see more clearly. By the time she turns him over to his final guide, the saintly Bernard, she has become unnecessary in Dante's life and spiritual development and can return to her blessed rest. This human love that she represents can lead people to God because it images forth his love. Not seeking oneself, like the proud, not desiring to possess another, like the lustful, the true lover is content to lead the pilgrim upward and to release him to the waiting hands of God.[24] In Beatrice's person and in her actions, we can easily see what Dorothy L. Sayers noted as the six gifts of love: worship, fear, beatitude, wonder, sorrow, and loss.[25]

The "Beatrician movement" then is the movement of revelation. As Charles Williams has expressed it, it is a "moment of choice. It is a choice between action and no action, intellect and no intellect, energy and no energy."[26]

Sayers' notes, which are her most impressive contribution to Dante scholarship, are full of the image of Beatrice and interpretations of her meaning. She sees her as an important and complex figure for Dante and for any Christian. She is:

> the Image of the Host. . . . Beatrice is the particular type and image of the whole sacramental principle of which the Host itself is the greater

> Image. . . . In the literal sense, what Dante looks upon is Beatrice; but on the three allegorical levels . . . she is Sacrament. Morally (i. e. as regards the way of the individual soul) she is, to Dante and to each one of us, the manifestation of the Divine glory in whatsoever beloved thing becomes to every man his own particular sacramental experience. Historically (i. e. in the world of human society) she is the Sacrament of the Altar.[27]

Since Dante's images usually function on an many as five levels, his Beatrice can also be the Bride in the book of Revelation, the church, the Body of Christ, and a Florentine banker's wife whom Dante loved.

This beautiful girl who fascinated Dante and gave shape to his vision also fascinated Dorothy L. Sayers. No two more different women could be imagined. Separated by time, by culture, by interests, and by almost every aspect of existence, they appear to have shared only their sexual identity. Beatrice Portinari, living in thirteenth-century Florence, is remembered by nothing but Dante's love of her. This medieval lady, in her modest pose, the object of semi-religious veneration by her mystic poet, contrasts starkly with Dorothy L. Sayers, a modern, independent, outspoken British career woman. No lyric poems stand as a tribute to Sayers' physical beauty. She was no object of adoration, no subject for chivalric song. No passionate and mystical young poet saw her as his way to Christ. In fact, Dorothy Sayers, with her love of beauty and of religion and of art and of love itself, sounds a good bit more like Dante than his lady. She must often have thought that she would have been a terrific man.

But Beatrice gave shape to many of Sayers' own ideas and became during the last decade of her life an object of frequent contemplation. She was an affirmation of reality and of the experience of human love. As she acts to redeem Dante through her guidance, she becomes God-bearer and divine schoolmistress. Certainly, this had become for Sayers herself an increasingly obvious calling. Less and less was she inclined to see herself as an innovator, and more and more she recognized that she was a teacher—a divine schoolmistress.

She knew that scholars resented her intrusion into Italian studies with this vast and courageous work. She undertook it with all due modesty: since no poet of Dante's stature was currently available to translate and recreate his work, she would have to serve. She knew that she was not a genius, not a great poet. But she also knew, in all due modesty, that she was an expert at her craft and a clear thinker with a gift for language. Her main job was to bring her beloved Florentine to her contemporaries in a form they could enjoy, to make his thought and form and experience available to them.

Like Miriam, Dorothy L. Sayers finally came to terms with herself. Moses' sister had been a poet and a prophet, always overshadowed by her brothers. Only at the end of her life did she let her resentment flash out. Then she accepted God's sharp answer and learned to live with her role in his world. When a woman has so much talent and so much energy, she can scarcely help resenting her ridiculous limitations. To be on the edge of greatness but never to be great is a special kind of anguish—the pain of Tantalus. It was also the pain of Moses and Miriam, who could see the promised land but not cross over into it. Sayers stretched herself as far as she could, only to acknowledge that hers was the secondary gift of interpreting. Unlike Dante, she could not speak powerfully of her own life, her own vision of God. Like Miriam, she was destined to find her blessedness in service. Her enthusiastic acceptance of this role made her final decade a blessed climax to a life of struggle.

This woman who had rejected the job of teaching young girls at the beginning of her life found herself a teacher of a whole nation at the end. As she noted in comments on her plays, she was using truth, rather than whimsy. She did not seek to be original, for the Scripture and the church fathers were most often her intellectual and spiritual guides. But she did think them profound. For her, what Beatrice provided for Dante and what she herself felt called upon to provide for others was an example of the "feeling intellect." Not the rationalism and artistry of Vergil (the classic artist), nor yet the pure spiritual insights of St. Bernard (the religious mystic); Beatrice (and Sayers) sought the middle way. Hers was the world of experience, human love and life, leading to the eternal experience of God's love.

In this final work, Sayers turned to Dante as Dante himself had turned to Vergil, in delight at a master craftsman. As a woman, she was fascinated by his use of the "otherness" of woman in the life of a man, a parallel experience to her own love of men. As an artist and a medieval, Dante thrilled her and enticed her into explorations of ideas and images she had long neglected. Intellectually as well as artistically, in Dante she found herself happily at home. Her scholarly and artistic career, her long musings on her own nature and her own life, her love of the intellect, and her great faith all made this final study one of the richest parts of her heroic life.

Dante's loneliness and exile echoed Sayers' own. She too was an outcast from her beloved city for much of her life—visiting Oxford only as a celebrated guest, not as a citizen. Like him, she reaped the bitter harvest of a changing world. The excitement of living in a new age of scientific progress and artistic experimentation was offset by the discomfort of uncertainty and stress. She, like Dante, turned to tradition as an anchor to balance change, experimenting with new forms while respecting the old. She, like him, tried to reconcile the new philosophy with the enduring faith, the theories with the life experience.

But she had a special struggle that the old Florentine could not share. She was a woman, trying to reconcile the traditional role of woman with the new sense of liberation. No other time in history has seen woman so torn by conflicting views of duty as our century. And Dorothy L. Sayers was at the cutting edge of the change—in the first class of Oxford women graduates, among the first women in the professional world, one of the first women playwrights and translators. At each step, she was judged first as a woman, then as an artist. She was never allowed to forget that she was "only" a woman. If she became occasionally overzealous in her struggle or strident in her tone, she certainly had justification. Yet she tried to maintain balance, to refrain from angry assertions about women's rights. Her intellectual integrity demanded that she be judged as an individual performing a job, not a woman proving she could do "man's" work. She was not just any woman; she was Dorothy L. Sayers. And this was not "man's" work; it was hers, assigned by God himself.

Because of her steady insistence on the vocation of the individual Christian, she never had the comradeship afforded by the women's movement to sustain her and lessen her loneliness. Hers was the solitary path of the exile from collective thought. The fiercely independent thinker pays the price, in any society. Sayers laughed at the way her world at one moment found her ridiculous and at another described her as courageous. She had not changed; the world had. She never shared her path for long with a congenial traveling companion, but then

Bunyan's pilgrim also found himself frequently alone. Even Evangelist stayed with him only a short time.

Christiana, of course (the good pilgrim's wife who followed with her children soon after he left home), had her children to take with her. But Sayers could never be content with this traditional feminine role. She followed neither husband nor son, relied on them barely at all for strength. She assumed the man's role of provider and decision-maker, not because she wanted to be manly, but because she saw a job that she needed to do. But she could not escape from her femininity entirely. She was invariably judged by the shape of her body and the condition of her clothing, as a man seldom is so exclusively. She delighted in her ability to fit into the same robes as G. K. Chesterton, but others sneered that she was outrageously fat. Her occasional efforts at a dashing appearance hint that she was aware of the criticism. But she generally opted for comfort and convenience over aesthetic appeal. Her favorite choice was her academic gown with the soft cap, symbolizing her proudest accomplishment rather than her sexual identity.

In a far deeper sense, her life and her spiritual history are thoroughly feminine. Though she found herself excluded from a happy marriage and satisfying motherhood, she noted in letters to friends that she was built for such a life. Because she was a woman, she lived from one opportunity to another, not planning her life as a grand adventure, but responding to the perils and closed doors and flowering meadows. She did not prepare for a profession or set goals for her career. That she moved so far so fast suggests her enormous talent and energy. Compare her career with the smoother and more sustained one of C. S. Lewis (as revealed in *Surprised by Joy*) to see how much straighter a path he followed, how easily he moved into scholarship and gathered congenial friends.

Nor had her life the dramatic confrontations and temptations of a man's. She knew neither the horrors nor the camaraderie of war. She knew only the anguish and pain of the survivors. Contrast her pitiful, furtive experiments in lust with St. Augustine's coming to Carthage "burning." She could look back at this great saint with his vast learning and violent emotions, his ties to family, his illegitimate child, and feel real kinship. But she could not match his great conversion experience and his public renunciation of pagan vices.

Hers was the milder, calmer career of the female saint, who finds no dramatic moments of change. The dark night of the soul transforms by gradual and indiscernible degrees into the brilliant dawn of God's illumination. This flowerlike unfolding of life is very different from the dramatic changes in a man's life. We can see in Dorothy Sayers' youth the seeds of those ideas and traits which blossomed forth in her life. Curiously, she often associates her modified self-portrait (Harriet Vane) with flowers and gardens. And looking back at her own life, she saw an organic unity in it. At one time, she quoted an early poem, noting that the ideas expressed in it were almost the same as those which appear in her mature works. She never had a blinding light from heaven turn her back from old ideas and old sins.

The faith she learned in her childhood provided the firm foundation for her mature faith. She gradually exchanged pap for "strong meat" as each phase of her life challenged her to grow yet stronger. By the time she came to her final works, she could describe a life flooded with love, but we cannot point to the moment when that light first entered her world.

Her landscape was less the depths and heights of Dante's or Bunyan's than the flat grid of the fen country, with high places reserved for God's house. In an article she wrote years after her life there, she described the silent tides of the cold North Sea, waiting to "reclaim their own," like some great monster out of prehistory. Lyrically, she noted, "The great Fenland churches, with their lofty bell-towers, stand today, as they stood of old, calling to one another across a waste of waters. If ever the dykes crumble away those churches may be the only part of the Fenman's defence against the water that will not have to be made over again."[28] She clearly saw herself as a "Fenman" (person?) facing the irrational and inhuman forces that threaten to claim our lives and our institutions. The church was to her the single solid structure in her threatened world.

In the long run, she was neither Beatrice nor Dante any more than she had been Lord Peter or Harriet. She was a little of each. She could not be the glorious lover or the bold sinner in such vivid and open terms as they. She saw something of herself in each of them, most of all perhaps in Dante. For she perceived herself as a great sinner, hardly realizing she had become a great and loving God-bearer as well.

The final decade of her life was given over to the translation and interpretation of Dante. She wrote innumerable letters and notes, she made many speeches to audiences infected with her zeal for this masterpiece, and she found that the first two volumes (Hell, Purgatory) sold more copies of Dante than ever before in history. She became, like Beatrice, the divine schoolmistress to a generation of young scholars—especially in America where her translations are a part of the curriculum in hundreds of colleges.

It is fitting and touching that, as Dante had died in the writing of *Paradiso*, Dorothy L. Sayers died in the translating of it. Nothing could be more appropriate than that Dante should have been the culminating experience in her rich and vital life. Like Beatrice, she handed the unfinished job over to another, in her case to her friend and colleague Dr. Barbara Reynolds, who prepared the notes for and completed the translation of the final section of *Paradiso*. For one who was ever self-reliant (like William of Sens, architect of Canterbury), the final lesson Sayers had to learn was to be forced to rest on others, and finally to rest in God. It is as if the exploding magnificence of the vision of God transfigured and tempted both Dante and Sayers out of the life of the flesh into the direct experience of the spirit.

On Tuesday, December 17, 1957, Dorothy L. Sayers, after a day of Christmas shopping, died in her home in Witham. She apparently died of coronary thrombosis, but she would have said that such facts are of no importance. The truth lies in the work she did, work that lives today with unaltered vitality. It seems good that she died in the midst of her greatest discovery, contemplating her greatest love, using her finest gifts, doing her proper work. An energetic soul to the end, thoughtful of others, eager to serve a greater artist than herself, and in serving him to serve the Great Master of all, she died full of plans for the next day. She must have realized that her health was failing, for she had made arrangements that the work continue without her, but according to her design.

Her final miles on the pilgrimage were magnificent—the best of life, for which the first was made. She made of old age a triumph, a fulfillment of promises, a harvest of mature thought. Following her love of a human master and of the divine one, drawing together through love friends and readers, she attained a synthesis of her life and ideas. Looking back over her life she could see her failures and mistakes. The whole path was finally clear, but she did not look back for long. To the very end, she looked forward, knowing full well that the great adventure lay just beyond the threshold of death.

At her funeral, mourners read her words from the essay "The Greatest Drama Ever Staged," her response to the Easter story. The panegyric by C. S. Lewis was read by the Bishop of Chichester. Five other bishops attended. Val Gielgud, who had produced *The Man Born to Be King*, read the first lesson. Countless friends mourned her passing. But no one doubted that she had stepped graciously through the gateway of death into the Celestial City she had spent her final year contemplating. She was home at last.

Her ashes lie in the tower of St. Anne's Church, in the bombed-out section of bohemian London, Soho. A society founded to study and remember her has placed a plaque there, inscribed: "The only Christian work is a good work well done."

Friends and readers of Dorothy L. Sayers continue to meet several times a year, to discuss her work, to commemorate her life. At one such Commemoration Service, held at St. Nicolas Church, Chipping Hill, Witham, November 27, 1976, the Reverend Aubrey Moody prayed this lovely prayer:

> Most merciful Father, we commend to Thee the soul of Thy servant Dorothy Leigh Sayers. We give thanks to Thee for her life, for her courage, for her kindness, for her faith, for her service to others, for her talents of wisdom and knowledge, for her gifts of interpretation and for all she was able to do to increase the meaning and beauty of life. O Father through whose love we live, wrap Thou Thy tenderness about her name; receive her life's offering and grant her light, blessing and peace for evermore.[29]

It is a fitting tribute for a pilgrim who joyed in her Christian work, and who came through human love to a discovery of the transcending love of God.

Works of Translation and Criticism

1929	*Tristan in Brittany (Le Roman de Tristan)*
1947	"'And Telling You a Story': A Note on *The Divine Comedy*" (in *Essays Presented to Charles Williams*, ed. C. S. Lewis)
1949	*The Comedy of Dante Alighieri the Florentine*, Cantica I, *Hell (Inferno)*
1954	*Introductory Papers on Dante*
1955	*The Comedy of Dante Alighieri the Florentine*, Cantica II, *Purgatory (Purgatorio)*
1957	*The Song of Roland (La Chanson de Roland)*
	Further Papers on Dante

Posthumous

1962	*The Comedy of Dante Alighieri the Florentine*, Cantica III, *Paradise (Paradiso)*, with Dr. Barbara Reynolds
1963	*The Poetry of Search and the Poetry of Statement* (essays)

Notes

Introduction

1. Roderick Jellema, "Introduction" to Dorothy L. Sayers, *Christian Letters to a Post-Christian World* (Grand Rapids, Mich.: Eerdmans, 1969), p. viii.

Chapter I. Pilgrim of the Intellect

1. Dorothy L. Sayers, "To M[uriel] J[aeger]," *Op I* (Oxford: Basil Blackwell, 1916), p. 70.
2. Dorothy L. Sayers, *Busman's Honeymoon* (New York: Harper & Row, 1937), chapter V, p. 92.
3. Jellema, "Introduction" to *Christian Letters to a Post-Christian World*, p. vii.
4. Dorothy L. Sayers, "A Vote of Thanks to Cyrus," *Christian Letters to a Post-Christian World*, p. 49.
5. Jellema, "Introduction," p. viii.
6. Dorothy L. Sayers, *The Nine Tailors* (New York: Harcourt, Brace & World, 1934), Fifth Part, p. 128.
7. Ivy Phillips in a letter to Mr. Clarke of the Sayers Society, 8 October 1977—available in the archives at the Roslyn House, Witham, Essex.
8. Ralph E. Hone, *Dorothy L. Sayers: A Literary Biography* (Kent, Ohio: Kent State University Press, 1979), p. 191.
9. Dorothy L. Sayers, *Gaudy Night* (New York: Harper & Row, 1936), chapter VIII, p. 171.
10. *Ibid.*, chapter VIII, p. 160.
11. *Ibid.*, chapter VIII, p. 162.
12. *Ibid.*, chapter IV, p. 77.
13. James Brabazon, "Dorothy L. Sayers: Player of the Game," speech at Wheaton College, 21 April 1978.
14. Dorothy L. Sayers, "Laughter," *Op I*, p. 66.
15. See Alzina Stone Dale's comments in *Maker and Craftsman: The Story of Dorothy L. Sayers* (Grand Rapids, Mich.: Eerdmans, 1978), p. 41, and her review of Charis [Barnett] Frankenburg's memoirs, *Not Old, Madam, Vintage*, in *The Sayers Review* II, 2 (June 1978), p. 25.
16. *Gaudy Night*, chapter III, p. 48.
17. *Ibid.*, chapter II, pp. 29–30.
18. *Ibid.*, chapter I, p. 10.
19. See Vera Brittain, *Testament of Youth* (New York: Macmillan, 1933), p. 508.
20. "To M[uriel] J[aeger]," *Op I*, p. 70.

Chapter II. Vanity Fair

1. "The Reluctant Lord Peter: Interview with Eric Whelpton," *Braintree and Witham Times*, 9 June 1976.
2. *Busman's Honeymoon*, chapter V, p. 92.
3. Dorothy L. Sayers, *Murder Must Advertise* (New York: Harper & Row, 1933), chapter XI, p. 180.
4. *Ibid.*, chapter III, p. 34.
5. Dorothy L. Sayers, *Are Women Human?* (Grand Rapids, Mich.: Eerdmans, 1971), p. 20.
6. *Murder Must Advertise*, chapter V, p. 74.
7. *Ibid.*, chapter XI, p. 180.
8. Dorothy L. Sayers, "The Other Six Deadly Sins," *Christian Letters to a Post-Christian World*, pp. 142–143.
9. *Ibid.*, pp. 144–145.
10. *Murder Must Advertise*, chapter XV, p. 243.
11. Dorothy L. Sayers, "Maher-Shalal-Hashbaz," *Hangman's Holiday* (London: Gollancz, 1975), p. 244. Quoted by permission of Armitage Watkins, Inc.
12. *Maker and Craftsman*, pp. 70–71.
13. "Proceedings" of the Dorothy L. Sayers Historical and Literary Society, Witham, Essex, 7 August 1977, p. 10.
14. "Proceedings" of the Dorothy L. Sayers Historical and Literary Society, Witham, Essex, 27 November 1976, p. 25.
15. Quoted at length by Dr. Margaret Hannay in her essay "Harriet's Influence on the Characterization of Lord Peter Wimsey," *As Her Whimsey Took Her*, ed. Hannay (Kent, Ohio: Kent State University Press, 1979), pp. 36–50.
16. Cf. "Aristotle on Detective Fiction," *Unpopular Opinions: Twenty-One Essays* (New York: Harcourt, Brace and Co., 1947), p. 231.
17. "Gaudy Night," *Titles to Fame*, ed. Denys Kilham Roberts (London: Thomas Nelson, 1937), pp. 79–80.
18. Janet Hitchman, *Such a Strange Lady: A Biography of Dorothy L. Sayers* (New York: Harper & Row, 1975), p. 69.
19. Dr. Barbara Reynolds, "Dorothy L. Sayers and the Art of Detective Fiction," speech at Wheaton College, 30 September 1977. Used by permission.
20. Dorothy L. Sayers, "The Present Status of the Mystery Story," *London Mercury* 23 (November 1930), p. 48.
21. *Ibid.*, pp. 47–52.
22. Dorothy L. Sayers, "A Sport of Noble Minds," *Life and Letters To-Day* 4 (January 1930), pp. 41–54.
23. See Dorothy L. Sayers, *Whose Body?* (New York: Harper & Row, n.d.), chapter VII, pp. 155–156.
24. *Ibid.*, chapter VII, p. 159.
25. Cf. Nancy-Lou Patterson, "Images of Judaism and Anti-Semitism in the Novels of Dorothy L. Sayers," *The Sayers Review* II, 2 (June 1978), pp. 17–24.
26. James Brabazon, "Dorothy L. Sayers: Player of the Game," Speech at Wheaton College, 21 April 1978.
27. *Ibid.*
28. See Ralph Hone, *Dorothy L. Sayers: A Literary Biography*, p. 44.
29. Hitchman, *Such a Strange Lady*, p. 46; Hone, *Dorothy L. Sayers: A Literary Biography*, p. 44.

Chapter III. Through the Valleys

1. John Bunyan, *The Pilgrim's Progress* (New York: Pocket Books, 1957), p. 92.
2. Dorothy L. Sayers, *Clouds of Witness* (New York: Harper & Row, n.d.), chapter X, p. 178.
3. Dorothy L. Sayers, *Unnatural Death* (New York: Harper & Row, 1927, 1955), chapter XIX, pp. 228–230.
4. Dorothy L. Sayers, "The Human-Not-Quite-Human," *Are Women Human?*, p. 45.
5. *Unnatural Death*, chapter III, p. 37.
6. *Ibid.*, chapter III, p. 31.
7. Vera Brittain, *The Women at Oxford* (London: G. G. Harrap, 1960), p. 30.
8. See "The Human-Not-Quite-Human," *Are Women Human?*, p. 47.
9. *Unnatural Death*, chapter XVI, p. 188.
10. *Ibid.*, chapter XVI, p. 184.
11. *Ibid.*, chapter XXII, p. 259.
12. James Brabazon, "Dorothy L. Sayers: Player of the Game," speech at Wheaton College, 21 April 1978.
13. *Ibid.*
14. Hone, *Dorothy L. Sayers: A Literary Biography*, p. 48.
15. "The Reluctant Lord Peter: Interview with Eric Whelpton," *Braintree and Witham Times*, 9 June 1976.
16. Dorothy L. Sayers, *The Unpleasantness at the Bellona Club* (New York: Harper & Brothers, 1928), chapter I, p. 6.
17. *Ibid.*, chapter XXIII, "Post-Mortem," p. 341.
18. *Ibid.*, chapter XXI, p. 322.
19. *Ibid.*, chapter XXIII, "Post-Mortem," p. 343.
20. *Ibid.*, chapter XV, p. 204.
21. Alzina Stone Dale, *Maker and Craftsman*, p. 79.
22. Reverend Aubrey Moody, "In Memoriam," *The Sayers Review* I, 2 (January 1977), p. 21.

Chapter IV. Pilgrim of the Heart

1. Dorothy L. Sayers, "Problem Picture," *Christian Letters to a Post-Christian World*, p. 114, Sayers' italics.
2. See Dorothy L. Sayers, *Have His Carcase* (New York: Harper & Row, 1932), chapter XVI, p. 211.
3. "Introduction" to *The Omnibus of Crime* (New York: Harcourt, Brace and Co., 1929), p. 14.
4. *Ibid.*
5. "Gaudy Night" in *Titles to Fame*, p. 81.
6. *Ibid.*, p. 86.
7. See Dr. Margaret Hannay, "Harriet's Influence on the Characterization of Lord Peter Wimsey," *As Her Whimsey Took Her*, pp. 36–50.
8. "Gaudy Night," *Titles to Fame*, p. 81.
9 *Ibid.*, p. 82.
10. *Ibid.*, p. 92.
11. *Gaudy Night*, chapter XIX, p. 395.

12. Dorothy L. Sayers, *The Mind of the Maker* (New York: Harcourt, Brace and Co., 1941), p. 131.
13. *Busman's Honeymoon*, chapter XIV, p. 248.
14. *Ibid.*, chapter XIV, p. 249.
15. "Dante and Charles Williams," *Christian Letters to a Post-Christian World*, p. 174.
16. *Busman's Honeymoon*, chapter XVI, p. 277.

Chapter V. On the King's Highway

1. Hitchman, *Such a Strange Lady*, p. 94.
2. Hone, *Dorothy L. Sayers: A Literary Biography*, p. 78.
3. *Ibid.*, p. 164.
4. Dorothy L. Sayers, *The Zeal of Thy House* in *Four Sacred Plays* (London: Gollancz, 1948), p. 47.
5. See "Introduction" to *The Zeal of Thy House* (London: Gollancz, 1937), p. 7.
6. *Ibid.*, p. 41. Quoted by permission of Armitage Watkins, Inc.
7. *Ibid.*, p. 42.
8. *Ibid.*, pp. 67–68. Quoted by permission of Armitage Watkins, Inc.
9. *The Just Vengeance* in *Four Sacred Plays*, p. 280.
10. *Ibid.*, p. 297. Reprinted by permission of David Higham Associates Ltd.
11. *Ibid.*, p. 280.
12. Hitchman, *Such a Strange Lady*, p. 124.
13. *Ibid.*, p. 135.
14. James Brabazon, "Dorothy L. Sayers: Player of the Game," speech at Wheaton College, 21 April 1978.
15. See Ralph Hone, *Dorothy L. Sayers: A Literary Biography*, pp. 113, 136; and Alzina Stone Dale, *Maker and Craftsman*, p. 118.

Chapter VI. The View from the Delectable Mountains

1. Lionel Basney, "Sayers and the 'Bonny Outlaw': Her Work as a Lay Apologist," paper delivered at the Dorothy L. Sayers Seminar, Modern Language Association, Chicago, 28 December 1977.
2. Dorothy L. Sayers, "Creed or Chaos?" in *Christian Letters to a Post-Christian World*, p. 44.
3. See Hitchman, *Such a Strange Lady*, p. 145; from a letter by Sayers to Dr. James Welch, 20 November 1943, in BBC archives.
4. Bulletin No. 12 of the Dorothy L. Sayers Society, September 1977.
5. "Creed or Chaos?" in *Christian Letters to a Post-Christian World*, p. 40.
6. See Dorothy L. Sayers, "Towards a Christian Aesthetic," *Unpopular Opinions: Twenty-One Essays*, pp. 41–43.
7. "Strong Meat," *Christian Letters to a Post-Christian World*, pp. 18–19.
8. Dorothy L. Sayers, "The Human-Not-Quite-Human," *Are Women Human?*, p. 47.
9. "Creed or Chaos?" in *Christian Letters to a Post-Christian World*, p. 39, Sayers' italics.

Chapter VII. The Celestial City

1. *Gaudy Night*, chapter XI, p. 229.
2. Dr. Barbara Reynolds, "Dorothy L. Sayers: Her Educational and Literary Ideals," lecture at Wheaton College, 29 September 1977. Used by permission.
3. Hitchman, *Such a Strange Lady*, p. 156.
4. "Introduction" to *The Comedy of Dante Alighieri the Florentine*, Cantica I, *Hell*, trans. Dorothy L. Sayers (New York: Basic Books, 1962), p. 36.
5. *Ibid.*, p. 39; taken from *Paradise*, XVII, pp. 55–60.
6. "Proceedings" of the Dorothy L. Sayers Historical and Literary Society, Witham, Essex, 27 November 1976, p. 43.
7. Paul De Voil, "Dorothy L. Sayers as a Theologian," speech at a seminar of the Dorothy L. Sayers Historical and Literary Society, Witham, Essex, 16 July 1978.
8. Dorothy L. Sayers, *Further Papers on Dante* (London: Methuen, 1957), p. 42.
9. *Ibid.*, p. 104. Used by permission.
10. Cf. Barbara Reynolds and James Brabazon, "Was She Such a Strange Lady?" duologue at Wheaton College, 22 April 1978.
11. "What Is Right with Oxford," *Oxford* II, 1 (Summer 1935), p. 41.
12. Reverend Aubrey Moody, "In Memoriam," *The Sayers Review* I, 2 (January 1977), pp. 22–23.
13. See her "The Poetry of Search and the Poetry of Statement" and "The Translation of Verse" in *The Poetry of Search and the Poetry of Statement* (London: Gollancz, 1963), pp. 7–19 and 127–153.
14. Alzina Stone Dale, "*The Man Born to Be King:* Dorothy L. Sayers' Best Plot," *The Sayers Review* I, 2 (January 1977), p. 5.
15. "Dorothy L. Sayers: Her Educational and Literary Ideals," lecture at Wheaton College, 29 September 1977.
16. *The Comedy of Dante Alighieri the Florentine*, Cantica III, *Paradise*, trans. Sayers, XXXIII, pp. 139–145. Used by permission.
17. Alzina Stone Dale, *Maker and Craftsman*, pp. 103–104.
18. *The Comedy of Dante Alighieri the Florentine*, Cantica II, *Purgatory*, trans. Sayers, XXXIII, p. 145.
19. *Further Papers on Dante*, p. 189.
20. *Ibid.* ·
21. *Ibid.*, p. 187.
22. *Ibid.*, p. 203.
23. *Ibid.*
24. See Sayers' introduction to *Purgatory* (Cantica II of *The Comedy*), p. 36.
25. *Further Papers on Dante*, p. 159.
26. Charles Williams, *The Figure of Beatrice* (New York: Farrar, Straus & Giroux, 1961), p. 123.
27. *Further Papers on Dante*, p. 192.
28. Dorothy L. Sayers, "The Fen Floods: Fiction and Fact," *The Spectator* CLVIII, 5675 (2 April 1937), pp. 611–622.
29. Bulletin No. 8 of the Dorothy L. Sayers Society, February 1977, p. 2.

Index